Creating Digital Illusions

Creating Digital Illusions

THE BLACKMAN PORTFOLIO

by Barry Blackman

VAN NOSTRAND REINHOLD

ITP® A Division of International Thomson Publishing Inc.

New York • Albany • Bonn • Boston • Detroit • London • Madrid • Melbourne
Mexico City • Paris • San Francisco • Singapore • Tokyo • Toronto

Cover design: Paul Costello
Cover art: Barry Blackman

Van Nostrand Reinhold staff:

Editor: Jane Degenhardt
Production Editor: Carla M. Nessler
Production Manager: Mary McCartney
Typesetter: Paul Costello

Book Design by Barry Blackman

I(T)P® A division of International Thomson Publishing, Inc.
The ITP logo is a registered trademark under license

Printed in Hong Kong

For more information, contact:

Van Nostrand Reinhold
115 Fifth Avenue
New York, NY 10003

Chapman & Hall GmbH
Pappelallee 3
69469 Weinheim
Germany

Chapman & Hall
2-6 Boundary Row
London
SE1 8HN
United Kingdom

International Thomson Publishing Asia
221 Henderson Road #05-10
Henderson Building
Singapore 0315

Thomas Nelson Australia
102 Dodds Street
South Melbourne, 3205
Victoria, Australia

International Thomson Publishing Japan
Hirakawacho Kyowa Building, 3F
2-2-1 Hirakawacho
Chiyoda-ku, 102 Tokyo
Japan

Nelson Canada
1120 Birchmount Road
Scarborough, Ontario
Canada M1K 5G4

International Thomson Editores
Seneca 53
Col. Polanco
11560 Mexico D.F. Mexico

1 2 3 4 5 6 7 8 9 10 CP-HK 02 01 00 99 98 97 96

Library of Congress Cataloging-in-Publication Data

Blackman, Barry, 1941-.
    Creating digital illusions : the Blackman portfolio / by Barry Blackman.
       p.   cm.
    ISBN 0-442-02141-0
    1. Computer graphics.   I. Title.
T385.B568   1996
778--dc20   96-15491
                                                                CIP

DEDICATION

To Carmen,

For putting up with all those lonely times when we've been forced to be

apart; for being a great mother to our two wonderful children,

Tara and Hillary; and especially for always being there by my side

when I needed you, I thank you with all my heart.

Your support, sacrifice, patience, love, and understanding,

has made this book possible.

To you, Carmen, the love of my life, the mother of my children,

and my best friend, I dedicate this book.

CONTENTS

ACKNOWLEDGMENTS

There are so many people to thank for their help, patience, and support in creating this book, that it would take a book to include them all. But, the following deserve a very special mention.

I met Yves Vanhauwaert when he first arrived in this country to introduce the Barco Creator in 1985. We discussed a book project then, but it was too early in the development of the industry. Over the years, his enthusiastic support and friendship has been invaluable to me personally and professionally. This book, in a way, is the result of his support and friendship.

Peter Loft, the guru of Barco Graphics, has taught me most of what I know about the Creator. But most important of all, whether in the United States or Belgium, he has never let me down when I have had a problem with the system or producing an effect that was outside the norm. Several images in this book would not have been as successful as they are without his help. I am grateful for his friendship.

To Chris DeJonge and Jason Harvey at Barco Graphics, Inc., U.S.A., thanks for your help throughout the project.

I want to thank Connie Miller, at Silicon Graphics Inc., for her unqualified support for this project. Her belief in this project helped tremendously in making this book become a reality.

John Cicchetti, a very talented computer artist and friend, was able to retrace the steps that I used to produced many of the image case histories in this book. Thanks, John, for your significant contribution to this project.

My thanks to Paul Foley at Image Axis. We go back along way, and I want to thank him and his crew of professionals: Willie Williamson, C.D.; Sean Barry; Robert Poole; et al for their wonderful service and for doing such a fantastic job in outputting all the chromes that were used in the production of this book.

To Nancy Wechsler, for doing such a capable job in protecting my interests, and for her friendship, my heartfelt thanks.

In all my dealings with the publishing industry, I have never worked with a more cohesive, knowledgeable, and enthusiastic team of professionals than I have had the privilege to be associated with at VNR. Thanks and kudos for a job well done to Jane Degenhardt, Beth Harrison, Carla Nessler, Paul Costello, Mary McCartney, and Cynthia Biron.

Most of all to my daughters, Tara and Hillary, my deepest love and gratitude for being so understanding of all the hours away from you.

And a special thanks to the rest of my family who have been so supportive through the years, I love you all.

Creating Digital Illusions

INTRODUCTION

"The future ain't what it used to be!"—Yogi Berra

WHY I GOT INVOLVED — A Personal Recollection

"Flu or no flu, I was not going to miss a personal demonstration of a high-end graphic computer workstation. I had been following the development of the graphic computer since I became aware of its existence in 1980. Finally, in 1985, the promise of a workstation that could output manipulated images on transparency film was a reality(or so I was told.

"Arranging this demo was not without great scheduling difficulty. I was in the middle of creating a complex surreal photo-illustration in the darkroom. The deadline was tight, but I was not going to miss this demonstration.

"It wasn't merely the showcasing of a new piece of equipment, at least not to me. I was a caveman who rubbed two sticks together for a week to make fire, about to see a cigarette lighter that could enable me to make that same fire in seconds. Walking into the computer room made me feel like Orville Wright venturing into the cockpit of a 747 airliner.

"Oblivious to my flu, I sat in wrapped attention as image after image was drawn from the computer's memory bank and manipulated. All were changed or enhanced quickly, easily, and differently. Some were stretched. Some were rotated. Others were color shifted or superimposed one on the other. Images were dissolved one into the next. They were posterized, solarized, masked, and joined. Still other photographic images were made into patterns, mirror imaged, and manipulated in countless other ways with a seeming flick of the wrist. One impossible image after the other materialized on the monitor screen.

"The demo was over. I left the future, a caveman returning to his cave to continue rubbing his two sticks together to make fire. The darkroom would never hold the same magic for me.

"As I walked the streets on the way back to my studio, the apparent oppressive truth weighed heavily on me. The demise of the special effects photographer, as I knew him, was inevitable.

"The press photographer of old carried a 4x5 Speed Graphic camera with his jacket pockets stuffed with flash bulbs and film holders. Today he has been replaced by a photojournalist with a couple of 35 mm cameras hanging from his neck and a padded nylon bag containing his film, lenses, and a strobe swinging from his shoulder. The special effects photographer would be replaced by the digital photographic illustrator. The equipment is different, the name has been changed, the results are better, but the job is the same.

"There will always be a need for a visualizer(one who can see images that do not exist and can make them exist on film as if they are real. I had to take the next evolutionary step, and I would need this marvelous electronic tool box to do it. It was clearly the tool of the visual industry's future."

THE FUTURE IS NOW

It is the future. For the first time in more than 150 years of photographic history, the computer gives the photographer the freedom to create or alter the photographic image without regard for the laws of physics or existing conditions. A freedom that painters have enjoyed for centuries is finally available to the photographer.

The computer's impact has sent ripples throughout the industry. Traditional retouchers have disappeared as suddenly and completely as the dinosaurs did. Unless they went digital, they went into some other line of work. Disappearing, too, are paste-up artists, comp artists, and typographers. Even color separation houses are feeling the pressures of obsolescence. Some of the effects of this digital revolution have not yet been realized. It is revolutionizing the way we think about photography(its veracity, its limitations, its direct relationship to literal existence, and its function as a credible chronicle of historical fact.

Its limits as a creative tool are now defined only by the imagination and creativity of the artist, photographer, designer, or art director. The ability to illustrate concepts and ideas with the impact of the implied reality photography represents is one of the tremendous strengths of the graphic computer. Never has the photographic image been so pliable and malleable. Never have the final results of manipulating an image been so predictable, nor have the post-photography changes to the image been so expansive and imperceptible. It can exaggerate object proportions, create perspective, merge and alter an infinite number of images, combine art with photography, and selectively alter or eliminate color.

In today's world, no creative person can ignore what is happening in and to this industry. The "creative" who knows and masters the capabilities that the graphic computer holds in its deceptively simple box will shine above his peers.

WHAT, WHY, AND HOW?

The electronic process of image altering is as miraculous today as the original image-capturing chemical process was 150 years ago. Traditional photography is the capture of light, reflected or transmitted, on a photo-sensitive emulsion. The reaction to light of the sensitized crystals in the gelatin emulsion is made visible by the chemical developing process. Frozen in the now visible image is a representation of a fraction of a second in the continuum of time: a somewhat factual portrayal of a section of the whole (an object, person, or situation) at a specific moment in time that will never exist exactly that way again. Until recently, the basic process has not changed.

With the advent of computer technology and the ability to convert light into numbers through a process called digitization, that frozen moment in the continuum can remain frozen or become a fluid part of a process in creating a faux reality. Just as light hitting the crystals in a film's emulsion causes changes that register the image, light striking a photo-sensitive silicon chip creates a reaction that generates numerical equivalents of the color and tonal values that embody the image. These numerical equivalents are in a digital language that the computer can read and understand. The computer is able to reconstruct the image on the screen from the numbers. At this point one can store the image in its digitized form for future recall since, unlike fragile film emulsion, it is immune to the deteriorating effects of time and environment. A second option is to manipulate the image in any way the artist desires, from simple retouching to complex overt changes.

How these changes are being made is deceptively simple. The computer rearranges the order of the numbers from which the image is constructed. This rearrangement is the result of the artist's use of a digitizing tablet or mouse to access the tools for image manipulation contained within the computer.

This photo-sensitive chip is contained in the two most common kinds of image capture devices: the scanner and the digital camera.

The scanner is used to digitize traditionally captured photographic images or artwork that enables the computer to work with them. High resolution images, digitized images containing billions and even trillions of numbers or "bits," are necessary to output or recreate on film the photographic looking image with its full tonal range and subtle details and nuances. The more digital information, the less evidence of computer involvement in producing the final image. Drum scanners are considered the highest quality, followed by flatbed scanners, and other forms of scanning devices.

Digital cameras or attachable camera backs that fit onto the standard camera body are other forms of image capture devices. In both devices, the digital camera and digital back, a computer coupled device chip (CCD) receives light at what would be the film plane in a traditional camera. Although the images are captured by scanners, the functionality of digital cameras and backs are becoming the photographic medium of choice for catalogues and photojournalism.

As computers become the norm in publishing and the graphic arts, the efficiency of photographing and digitizing simultaneously is very compelling for catalogue and magazine work. Since most photographs appearing in catalogues are relatively small, the low resolution of the image is less of a consideration. Secondly, since most images need a minimum amount of retouching and catalogues contain a great many images, a tremendous time and expense savings is realized by sending the images directly into the computer where they can be worked on without additional costs for film, processing, and digitization.

The imaging enhancement techniques developed by NASA for the computer allow a refinement of even the lowest resolution images from digital cameras to be brought up to a quality suitable for reproduction in newspapers or magazines. It is possible to take pictures half a world away on magnetic disc and send them immediately by modem to the graphic computer at the magazine, newspaper, or wire service. The image is enhanced until the quality is sufficient for publishing. Eliminating the developing, printing, and shipping time makes it possible for the image to go to press, depending on the timeliness of the event, within a couple of hours after the picture has been taken. The photographer can then reuse the magnetic disc again to record new images. The advantages of digital cameras are incredibly strong but open a variety of issues that were nonexistent or of minimal importance before the digital revolution.

Some of the issues are unique to photojournalism, and some issues (ethical and legal) are raised by the capabilities of the photographic digital process in general. Copyright infringement, ownership, model releases, veracity relative to journalism, and the photographic image as evidence are some of the issues raised, and most are still awaiting testing in the courts.

Once the images have been brought into the computer and manipulated or retouched, they have to be converted back into a photographic image on paper, transparency, or separation negative film. The piece of equipment that makes the conversion from numbers to physical image is called an output. It can come in several forms: a paper proof, which is a low resolution image, that looks very much like a C print; a color or black and white transparency in an 11x14 inch, 8x10 inch, 4x5 inch, 120 mm, or 35 mm format; or separation negatives, which are the breakdown of a full color image into the four printing press colors (cyan, magenta, yellow, and black) in the form of a black and white film negative for each color that is used to make the press plate, which will print that color ink on the sheet of paper. The cumulative effect of the imprint of each color plate, one on the other, is a full- or four-color image on a sheet of paper.

THE BOTTOM LINE

The more knowledgeable the art director/designer is about the creative potential of a high resolution electronic imaging system, (how far he or she can push the manipulation, what effects and techniques are available for him or her to use, and what images it might be possible to create through the use of digital photographic illustration) the more freedom he or she will have to create and expand the visual possibilities of communication, impact, and aesthetics. This knowledge will also protect the creative person from mediocre imagery produced by an inept or uninspired operator.

The art director/designer can also consider the graphic computer his insurance policy. A "should have, could have, would have" reflection in light of a post shoot evaluation through the 20/20 view of hindsight is visually painful. At one time, an improvement over what was shot, such as a variation of a setup that would have worked better, a change in the color of the clothes that would work better for the mood or composition, the splash of liquid that should have been bigger, or the model that should have been standing in a different place for the layout would have to be weighed against the cost of doing the shot over again. Reshoot? Not necessarily! A great deal can be done with electronic imaging to save or create an image that the creatives of the advertising and editorial industry could not have considered until this technological miracle came into existence.

Another scenario that an art director/designer can identify with is one in which he or she wants to try an idea but is unclear about the subtleties of size relationships, distortion, or color. It is no problem for him or her to: make changes in real time; save alternate variations for later consideration; adjust and fine tune the image until it is perfect; see it on the screen before it becomes a transparency. Without the computer's ability to accomplish this and more, an art director would have to dismiss a unique idea as too much of a gamble and settle for a safer photo-illustration.

The function of this book is to show not only the techniques that are available, but how they were applied to solve creative problems in real world situations for real clients.

It should be noted that the majority of the photos presented in this book were shot by the author specifically for manipulation by the computer. Every image was created by the author on his own graphic workstation in his studio. Images were photographed with an understanding of how the computer uses the photographic information provided and what it needs to process the image in the most efficient way. It is only with an in-depth knowledge of the digital capabilities of the system and years of experience that the desired results were accomplished in the least amount of time. It is also knowing what is best captured by the camera and what is best produced in the most effective manner possible. An experienced digital photographic illustrator can take full advantage of the best capabilities that computers and photography have to offer.

A photographer's working knowledge of the graphic computer system on which the final image will be completed is invaluable to the client and the computer artist who must work with the photographic components.

To the client, it is worthwhile to carefully select a photographer because it can save a great deal of expensive time on the computer. In understanding the capabilities of the computer, the photographer can shoot more efficiently by spending time on areas that will appear in the final image rather than areas that would be best done on the system or eliminated when the image is created. This should translate into a less expensive shoot.

The computer artist can save time and unnecessary work by using images that were created with techniques to maximize time-saving functions in the graphic computer. The reduced photography and computer fees are a welcome benefit of the new technology in this age of the ever-shrinking budget.

For the photographer, shooting individual components means less work setting up the shot. The photographer has to only concentrate on the subject that is being shot. He or she now has the freedom to light it properly without worrying about reflections or shadows cast on nearby objects. The photographer only needs to be concerned with consistency of lighting and perspective in matching one component to the other components for assembly on the system.

The computer artist can silhouette even complex objects, if photographed properly, by masking out the background automatically, in seconds, instead of the time-consuming hand work usually associated with detailed silhouetting of complex objects. The resulting artwork is also superior because the individual components have been photographed to fit together.

With proper planning, appropriate grain relationships between the different components can be matched, a single point of view regarding camera angles and perspective can be achieved, and consistent lighting can be maintained throughout. The art director/designer and his or her client are the beneficiaries of the unique capabilities of each medium by achieving optimum results at the best possible price.

ABOUT THIS BOOK

What follows are case histories of actual projects and the step-by-step procedure that the author followed to create the desired image. Some of the assignments are for advertising, some are for editorial usage, and others are miscellaneous projects that were significant in the challenges they presented and the solutions they inspired.

The purpose of breaking down the creative process is to acquaint the reader with the technical possibilities that are available for problem solving. A second goal is to demonstrate their application in practical situations. Another function of the storyboard approach is to give an insight into the thought and the development process in creating each work.

Every art director/designer should know the process that he or she will be utilizing to realize their concepts. Computer artists should find the case histories a source for new or different ways of approaching their projects. Photographers should be familiar with the techniques that may be applied to their work after it leaves their hands. Students who are studying computer graphics should find this book a valuable insight into real world applications of the theory they are learning. Finally, those who are simply curious about the way the images they see in magazines and brochures are created, this book will answer many questions.

NOTES ON THE PRODUCTION OF THIS BOOK

This book was written in a non-technical and non-system specific format to allow everyone with image editing software or a graphic workstation the possibility of applying the techniques and processes described to their system and software.

Not every program will be able to duplicate all the techniques described herein directly, but most can be duplicated with "work arounds." It would be impossible to write specifically for every graphic paint box program on the market. Each has its own terminology and even its own unique names for tools that could be found on other systems. A cloning brush on one system, for example, is a transfer brush on another system. The masking system in one program may work differently than a similarly named masking system on another. Even the order of the steps in a process varies from one system to the next.

To overcome this problem of semantics, I described what the process I used was set out to accomplish, or how a tool that I used worked. In this way, you can apply the appropriate applications in the proper order, dictated by the way your system operates, to accomplish the same or similar results.

PHOTOGRAPHIC MATERIALS AND EQUIPMENT

The Chinese have a saying, "Even the longest journey starts with the first step." As it applies to the most complex digitally produced photo-illustrations, it begins with the photographic images. These are the bricks with which you build that final image. If the original images are of poor quality, it may be possible to disguise, correct, or even compensate for the image's shortcomings electronically, but rarely is it helpful to use inferior imagery.

Except as noted, all the pictures in this book were photographed by myself. In the belief that garbage in results in garbage out, I shot almost all of my images on Kodak Ektachrome Professional or Lumiere film. For the twenty five years in which I have used Kodak film professionally, Kodak has never let me down as regards product or service.

I use three basic film formats: 35 mm, 120 mm, and 4x5. The 35 mm system I use is a Nikon. I use a N90s body with a wide range of lenses. Because of the variety of lenses I must use, the conditions I find myself shooting under, and the unusual computer generated lighting situations I have to match, this camera, with its versatile metering and advanced auto focus capabilities, fills my needs perfectly.

The most ideal format for photo composition is the medium, or 120 mm format. It has a resolution that fits perfectly with 4x5 or 35 mm components. I've used a *Hasselbladtt* system for over twenty five years and am still amazed by the optical sharpness of their lenses and the durability of their equipment.

Large format and versatility are what made the Sinar Pro a perfect match for the often bizarre kind of images I have to produce. Their modular system has always worked well with the wide ranging demands that my kind of imagery calls for, going back twenty five years to the period before computers, when many effects were created in the camera.

COMPUTER HARDWARE AND SOFTWARE

When I first decided to make that leap of faith into the digital image manipulation genre, I tried several systems before settling on a Silicon Graphics Personal Iris workstation. It proved the truth of the adage, "You have to kiss many frogs before you find a prince." That was ten years ago. Since then, I moved up over the years through the S.G.I. Power Series 240 GTX to the S.G.I. Indy with a R4400 processor chip, 24 bit color, 150 MHZ processor, and 160 MB of RAM.

The software graphics package that I used then, as now, was and is Barco Graphic's Creator. Barco's ability to constantly upgrade and stay ahead of the pack with the most versatile and comprehensive graphics software package on the market today has left me with little need to look for additional software.

All the images in this book were created on my Silicon Graphics Systems with Barco software. Beyond the creation of individual images, all the single bleed pages in the book and the photographic spreads that contain the individual images were designed, the backgrounds created, and the assembly made on my system. The text was designed by the designer at the publisher and added at the separation stage during the production of this book.

To avoid any potential problems in the production of the book at the Hong Kong sight where it was produced, all the color photographic pages were made from separations of 8x10 transparencies created from files that were approximately 250 megabytes each. They were written onto Kodak transparency film by an LVT output device at Image Axis, a digital service bureau in New York City. The professionalism of their staff and the quality of their outputs under tremendous time pressure and volume, made a significant contribution to the beautiful reproductions of my images in this book.

THE BUILDING BLOCKS OF CONCEPT
Symbols, Colors, and Effects

Ominously in the darkness, the dense foliage of *Jurassic Park* that is walling in the stalled vehicles, is hiding but not restraining the unseen creatures that go bump in the night. In the faint light, the young boy looks, quizzically, at the soda cup sitting on the dashboard of the stalled jeep in which he had been riding. The only sound is the muffled machine gun-like staccato of the rain hammering on the metal roof. He's sitting with the engine off, watching the ripples rhythmically appearing and disappearing on the surface of the liquid in the cup. He listens carefully, aware that he is in the area of Jurassic Park where the dreaded T-Rex dinosaur dwells.

Director, Steven Spielburg knows how to setup an audience. In the context of this setup, the visual clue of the ripples in the soda cup enables the audience, based on their life experience, to tentatively draw two conclusions. The first is that it is vibrations caused by the impact of something big and powerful creating the physical reaction in the liquid and, second, T-rex is coming. It is night, dark and raining so that vision is limited, and their vehicles have stalled, narrowing their options for escape. All are symbols or are symbolic of being very vulnerable. Lightning flashes and rolls of thunder add two more omi-

Steven Speilberg

nous layers to the setup. The momentum of the mounting apprehension continues in the audience's mind. The more that is left to the audience's imagination as they connect the cues (symbols or triggers) and draw conclusions, the greater the anticipation. When another symbol is added, a low pounding sound in sync with the ripples, their conclusion becomes certain and the mental and emotional terror begins. Primed and ready, the audience waits breathlessly for the T-Rex to appear.

This technique of constructing a concept by laying one symbol upon another until the realization of the idea becomes inescapable is much more intriguing, involving, and intense (therefore memorable) than if there was no guess work or building of anticipation through the introduction of clues. What a difference it would have made to the unfolding of the scene if the dinosaur simply walked out of the trees?

9

Ingmar Bergman

In the movies, Ingmar Bergman, the Swedish director who directed *Virgin Spring*, *Wild Strawberries*, and *The Seventh Seal*, used visual symbols not only to build his story but to represent concepts that played on other levels, communicating secondary, although profound, meanings that underlie the basic story line.

The Italian director, Frederico Fellini, was much more overt in his use of symbolism. In his movies, *8½* and *Satiracon*, the bizzare imagery and unique symbology was so strong that soon the audience was made aware that they, not the plot that initially caught the audiences' interest, were the keys to the real story. Audiences would puzzle their meanings for days after seeing his films. The deeper meaning had to be divined by deciphering the visual clues that interacted with the story line and dominated his films.

Although the movies had more to work with, such as sound and time, the intriguing use of visual cues and clues work just as powerfully in the still image. The artist, the photographer, and most recently the digital imagist can draw on: Greek and Roman mythology, color and its subconscious effects on the human psyche, pagan symbols, clichés, metaphysics, traditional and modern icons, and unique manipulations of everyday images to build multilayered unique imagery that intrigues, dazzles, and puzzles the mind. They can create images that stay hauntingly in the memory or move the soul because they communicate on many different levels.

Frederico Fellini

Salvador Dali and Rene Magritte were masters in the use of the visual icon to communicate volumes of meaning beyond the simple image present on the surface of the canvas. They used pictures as words that speak volumes to the mind's eye. The melting pocket watches in Dali's painting, *Persistence of Memory*, have much greater meaning than a representation of plastic objects left in the heat too long. They were his metaphor for the visualization of time and space. Crutches and crucifixes were also an often used part of his visual vocabulary, which changed definition by the context in which they became an integral component. His imagery, like many other surrealists, dealt with what might be likened to dreamlike imagery or scenarios. The worlds he created bore no resemblance to the world at large, nor did the objects and creatures that inhabited those worlds have any familiarity. The net result, however, was hauntingly unforgettable imagery that made one ponder the meaning of not only the whole of the artwork but also the meaning of its parts.

Salvador Dali

Rene Magritte also used objects to make points that went far beyond their literal meaning. His images were less dreamlike. He used everyday objects, settings, and images. His images' profound impact was due in part to the contradictory and, sometimes, illogical blending of common objects that became uncommon visions. He created new worlds out of the one that people already knew. They were not ominous worlds, but fascinating ones because they were almost familiar. Instinctively, one had to look for a deeper or hidden meaning to these pictures that were almost normal. They inspired a belief that its meaning was just below the surface, almost obvious and decipherable.

Rene Magritte

M. C. Escher, on the other hand, created pictures that fooled the eye and teased the mind. His were worlds that had stairs that climbed back into itself and waterfalls that fell into the river that fed into the same waterfall from whence it came. It had rooms that defied gravity and fish that turned into birds. He used these optical tricks as symbols to connect and communicate his thinking with the viewer.

Jerry Uelsmann, a contemporary photographer, pushed the "outside of the envelope" using of symbols and iconography to create photographic imagery that generates a sense of awe and wonder. His trees floating with exposed roots over a lake are to photography as Dali's melted watches and burning giraffes were to painting. He was able to turn photographic images of people, places, and objects into icons that gave him a language with which to communicate his deepest, personal, and emotional thoughts.

M.C. Escher

What he was able to create within the limitations of the darkroom in black and white, the digital photographic imagist can now do without limits, in color. Painters, for centuries, have been able to create new realities on canvass without regard for the laws of nature and physics, and now, finally the digital photographic illustrator can do the same.

This symbolic language, which takes many forms, is drawn from life experience and the creative psyche. In religion, the visual cues are everywhere, with the greatest contributions made by the masters of the Renaissance. Raphael, Micheangelo, and DaVinci, to name a few, popularized auras and halos as the representation of piety or sainthood. Shafts of light from the heavens indicated divine communication. Clouds signified heaven, and an old but powerfully built Caucasian man with a long white beard represented God. The cross represented Christianity just as the six pointed star, called the "Star of David", symbolized Judaism and the five pointed star, the pentagram, symbolized Satanism. Buddhism, is most often represented by figures of Buddha, usually in a meditative cross-legged position. Because religion is rooted in legend, mythology, and history, and is based on faith, emotion, and superstition, it is almost impossible to create a visual without using symbols of one kind or another. The artists of the renaissance had few symbols to draw on in order to quickly communicate the awesome majesty of God, the holiness of saints, and the mystical experience

Jerry Uelsmann

of religion. They were forced to create their own icons and visual triggers that would evoke feelings of awe and reverence. Auras and halos became crowns, symbols of sainthood, of religious authority and royalty within a mythical religious social structure. They borrowed signs of power from the Greeks and Romans. The huge dark cumulous clouds with flashes of lightning have been symbols of divine residence, indicators of awesome power and, in some cases, representative of anger and punishment. Without the darkness and lightning, the large white cumulous clouds set in a blue sky created the landscape of heaven.

The use of visual symbology as an expression of mystical power, and a pictorial explanation of the unexplainable is traceable through time to the dawn of man. This need to communicate through imagery has been a basic drive within man since the beginnings of our existence. Religions, cultures, and societies around the world, from primitive cave paintings of prehistoric man to the Mayans to the Egyptians to the Chinese, have used pictures to communicate and record their histories, their cultures, and their beliefs. Pictures became hieroglyphics in Egypt and pictographs in China, which evolved into letters and, finally, into words.

The cave paintings of the Lascaux caverns in Dordogne, France, depicts a man as a stick figure, possibly representing a wounded hunter. Thin lines are his spears and throwing stick. Large depictions of mammoth, bison, horses, reindeer, boar, and wolf, it is believed, had some magical or mystical significance relating to the hunt. These were accurately detailed pictures (considering the artists rendered them by the light of crude oil lamps 850 yards deep inside the cave) of what they represented and the subject matter that they were trying to communicate. Communicate they did, and do, with the members of their group and with mankind today, 12 thousand to 17 thousand years later.

In the tombs of the Egyptian pharaohs, in the Valley of the Kings, were paintings of the lifestyle of the times, their gods, and their beliefs on how they were going to reach the hereafter. Within these pictures were symbols: the symbols of the pharaoh's power and authority. His head gear, the equivalent of his crown, and his scepter were both unmistakable trademarks of authority and position. His transportation to the afterlife was pictured as a boat. Anibus, god of embalming and protector of royal remains, was visualized as a figure that was half man, half jackal. In addition, the walls are covered with pictographs, hieroglyphics that are the language of symbols.

Starting with simple scratches made on stone or bark to communicate simple primitive messages to their primeval peers, man has always used symbols to convey meaning. As societies developed, first from families to small groups to tribes to nations, their need and ability to communicate more complex meanings and messages developed, too. Society became more complex. As society changed, technology, science, art, and literature expanded, and the medium of communication changed with it, evolving from cave paintings to hieroglyphics to the syllable picture writing of the Chinese and finally to the sound of today's alphabet. But even today, picture symbols are used everywhere and in every aspect of our lives for instant communication. Wordy concepts have to be analyzed, then visualized and associated or compared with references stored in our memories to discern its meaning. Symbols, icons, pictographs, signs, emblems, ideographs, and other visual triggers communicate more quickly, and on several levels simultaneously. It is a visual shorthand for an idea or ideas. Emotionally, intellectually, and subconsciously, a visual metaphor connects through the mental memory bank, and associations are made on all three levels. This connection makes visual symbology the optimum communication tool of the artist.

We use pictorial symbols in more ways than we are even aware. The human skull as an icon for death or mortal danger, for instance. Pirates used this symbol, known as the "Jolly Roger," on flags and pennants that adorned their ships to instill fear in the hearts of their prey. Now it is used to adorn bottles that contain chemicals that are poisonous if ingested. It is also a powerful component when used to introduce an ominous element to an image. An example might be the subtle suggestion of a skull's image in the smoke of a cigarette as it curls upward.

Pictograms, ideograms, or visual symbols can also change in meaning over time because of associations attached to it. The swastika, for example, was, for thousands of years, an oriental and native American Indian symbol for good luck and good fortune. The rise of the Third Reich, National Socialism, or as it is popularly known, Nazism, has made the symbol of the swastika, to western man, one of oppression and man's inhumanity to man. Any other meaning without specific references are buried. A hammer, symbol of the worker, when combined with the sickle, symbol of the farmer, became the trademark of tyranny and of world domination in the form Communism. The cross, the dreaded symbol of Roman punishment, has become the embodiment of Christianity.

The use of symbolism does not always have to be so overt in order to make its impact felt. Overall tonality, whether light or dark, creates a mood as does color or the lack of it. A light airy picture full of bright color inspires a feeling of freedom and a carefree atmos-

Life/Rebirth

bud (plant)	baby	sun	ocean	rain
tree	sunrise	stream	seedling	pregnant woman
egg	thumbs up	fish	candle	phoenix

Hope

prayer	white dove	shaft of light	open road	blue sky
white clouds	rainbow	woman	sun	candle

Death/Ending

human skull	tombstone	cross	desert	wreath
coffin	cattle skull	sunset	dark clouds	closed door
lily (flower)	blood	scythe	body outline	silhouette (figure)
crow	vulture	shadow	dead dove	thumbs down
	ace of spades	extinguished candle	traffic barrier	

Violence/Tragedy/Anger

broken glass	bloody knife	clenched fist	blood	police flasher
smoking gun	tears/crying	fire	explosion	road flare
bruised face	bandages	ambulance	mob	bicycle chain in fist
		bat/pipe		

Happiness/Celebration

confetti	party hats	smile	fireworks	champagne popping
toasting	streamers	hugging	tears	presents
blue sky	white clouds	laughter	applause	shoulder carry
bright colors	bright flowers	bouquet/roses	sun	light environment

Sadness/Dispair

tears	alcohol	drugs (illegal)	pills	darkened room
head in hands	empty space	flat gray sky	leafless tree	dark unlit house
rain	neutral/dark colors	dead rose	gray environment	

phere. Grayish blue cast overall, with few colors or subdued colors, will create a very somber mood regardless of what else is going on in the image.

There are enough symbols in common use today to fill a book by itself. The following is a sampling, a basis from which to create a more complete list.

When creating a conceptual image, unless there is a preconceived idea of where to start, begin with a symbol that encompasses the basic concept. Then expand the idea with other icons or triggers that will flesh out the concept's subtext. Visual cues (the use of color to establish background foreground relationships, mood, the environment, the beliefs, and the emotional feelings of the subject the artist wants the audience to feel when looking at the image that he or she has created) should be layered or subtly intertwined within the image.

The digital artist can now use the language of color with the same ease that he or she could use iconography to communicate on other levels, the subconscious being one of them.

Color has been scientifically proven to possess the powerful ability to affect a profound physical and emotional change on people, but, at present its use is at the surface level. With a pallet of 16.8 million colors available for use on computer—more than the human eye can discriminate—color's potential is practically unlimited. The application of the results of experimentation with, and the exploration of color as a tool of the artist and communicator has just begun.

COLORS

The incredible power of color has been relatively ignored by graphic designers, art directors, and photographers. Although the use of color is as much a science as an art, their primary interest in color has been aesthetically driven, ignoring the vast amount of scientific research concerning the physical, emotional, and visual affects and reactions of color on man. It is true that a great deal of this research is more appropriate to interior design, industrial design, and medical application than to artistic usage, but there remains a large amount of knowledge that is indeed applicable to the arts

It has been proven that the color red is capable of raising the pulse rate and blood pressure in people. The color blue has the opposite effect. It not only lowers blood pressure and pulse rate, but has a soothing, calming effect on hyper or aggressive behaviors. Green has been proven to promote and speed healing. Although this research is fascinating, its relevance to the graphic arts is limited. It is, therefore, necessary to consider the information gained as a result of scientific research on color along with the artistic observation of color.

The unappreciated significance and importance of color in art, aside from the purely aesthetic consideration, is in the context of its symbolic meaning, its psychological effect by association, and its emotional impact through subconscious interpretation.

A quick review of the basics regarding color may be helpful. The physics of transmitted colored light or white light traveling through a filter acts differently than white light bouncing off a colored surface, which is called reflected light. White transmitted light is the product of a combination of the three primary colors, also known as additive colors, red, blue, and green, in equal parts. Secondary or subtractive colors, cyan, magenta, and yellow, when combined in equal parts, produce black. The secondary colors are produced by mixing two of the three primary colors: red plus blue equals magenta; blue plus green equals cyan; and, surprisingly, red plus green equals yellow. The full visible spectrum of color produced from white light when broken up by a prism, from the shortest wavelength to the longest, is: red, orange, yellow, green, blue, indigo, and violet. Neutral green divides the spectrum in half between the cooler colors and the warmer colors.

It is the secondary colors, magenta, cyan, and yellow, and black that are used by the printing industry to reproduce colored photographs and artwork with full tonality. This is commonly referred to as four-color printing using a dot pattern to blend the four colors, in different ratios, to create the full spectrum of colors. Because printing inks are not pure color, the light reflected does not react the same way that transmitted light does. When you combine green and red colored inks, the resulting color is not yellow, but brown. Combining all three secondary color inks in equal parts, the resulting color is not black, but a muddy brown. Therefore, the only way to get black on the printed page is to use black ink, the forth color.

The most basic and general consideration when designing or composing an image, whether it be a montage, photo composition, or merely setting up a shot, is that color should appear as it does in nature.

Depth is an illusion that can be totally or partially created with color. When color manipulation is combined with optical effects such as blurring or focus, the resulting effect is a clear separation of planes. Add an effect of diminished saturation of color to objects or the part of the landscape that is supposed to be distant. Then give the color a shift towards the cooler end of the spectrum and you have created an effect in the image of vast distance. The creation of spatial illusion with color rely, partially, on visual experience for certain colors to suggest depth or distance. Red and the warmer colors have shorter wave lengths, and blue and the cooler colors of the spectrum have longer ones.

It is no coincidence that cooler colors tend to recede and warmer colors advance. There are physical reasons for this phenomena. The retina of the eye is covered with rods and cones(the light sensors, which not only sense light but define color. The rods, which are more sensitive to light and more sensitive to cool colors(which are imbued with longer wavelengths(are brought into play when the eye focuses on a distant point. Cones, which are warm or shorter wavelength sensitive, are used to register and interpret light when the eye focuses on a point that is closer. Therefore, the eye responds to warm and cool colors as it does when it focuses on a near or far point, and so, the brain interprets it accordingly.

To duplicate the effect of distance on light, more is required than just the knowledge that blue recedes and red comes forward. Spatial illusions with color partially rely on visual experience to suggest that certain colors indicate depth or distance. The four attributes of color that affect depth perception are: temperature (cool/warm), brilliance(light/dark), saturation (intensity/dullness), and field (color-area relationships).

Temperature. The colors with the shortest wavelengths(red, orange, and yellow(are the warm colors. Blue, indigo, and violet are the cool colors with the longest wavelengths. As light travels away from its source, the color changes towards the cooler hues because the shorter wavelengths fade first. The longer the distance or atmospheric resistance, the cooler the light. Distant mountains appear to be purple and underwater photographs, without supplemental lighting, have a definite bluish cast that gets stronger as the light travels deeper and the warmer colors lose the battle with the density of the water and disappear.

Brilliance. Brighter or lighter colors, regardless of its color temperature, will advance. Darker and duller colors will recede. A brightly colored object will always stand out against a bunch of darkly or neutrally colored objects, in part because of the contrast and in part because of the attribute of brilliance.

Saturation. Pure color will always advance more than adulterated color or colors without the intensity and fullness of pure color, even when the brilliance of those colors are the same. As the purity of the color diminishes through pastels and into grayish color, it recedes more. The farther it travels from the eye, the brightest and most vividly colored object will start to lose brilliance and become a hazy, almost grayish, version of the color it started as. Not only does it physically recede, but it appears to do so visually as its color fades, and over time, we learn to recognize this phenomena as an effect of distance.

Field. Color is a subtle phenomena and is only a dominate factor regarding depth or distance on a level playing field where all colors are treated equal. Even then, positioning is important. If the color field or object of a distinctly recessive color overlaps a color field or object that is of a color that would normally project forward, the overlapping object is generally pushed forward by the object or field in the background.

An image is affected more by physical laws of physics, its surroundings, or perspective than by its color. However, don't underestimate the contribution of color to the physical effect. It is as important an element in creating the effect of distance as perspective, albeit on a more subtle level. Color is at its most powerful in its ability to generate mood and emotion. Its use as a communication tool or medium is very much underrated. The symbolic content of color and its associations with all aspects of life was appreciated more by primitive man than by our sophisticated society today, even though it is used all the time in a great many ways that people aren't cognizant. Red for danger, yellow for caution, and green for go are three of the more obvious uses of color as communicators and symbols. Rarely are the less obvious symbolic meanings of color effectively put to use.

Color as symbology. The symbolism or meaning that is attached to specific colors affects the way we perceive objects and the images that we attach to them. A black dress is associated with formal evening wear and sophistication, or clothing for a funeral. In red, it can be a gaudy party dress or the uniform for a flirt or hooker. If it were white, it would be a wedding dress, confirmation dress, or christening gown, and depending upon the style, it could also be a nurse's uniform. Black for sophistication or death, red for passion or lust, and white for purity, virginity, piety, and in the last case, sanitation and medical care. Some associations are universal and others are distinctly societal. Some associations are easily understandable, and others are not as apparent, such as purple signifying royalty, which has an obvious root in tradition. The separation isn't always so clear as is the situation with the color white, which symbolizes death to the Chinese. These are not the only symbolic associations or meanings for these colors. A list of them is at the end of this section.

The psychological and symbolic language of color cannot be specifically defined because colors derive their meaning from a number of different sources. They derive their meaning from and are modified by personal experience, cultural teachings, and societal custom. When combined with other visual cues such as icons, shapes, and objects, color then becomes a communicator of more specific concepts and deeper meaning.

This knowledge of the symbolism and emotions generated by specific colors enable the art director to communicate with a target market on a subconscious and obviously subtler level. This awareness of color meaning can also help him or her avoid the pitfalls of hitting sensitive hot buttons for specific industries or clients that would elicit a negative response. An ad was designed and executed for a campaign for Citibank utilizing red and orange streaks to simulate laser beams. Running the comps (mock-ups of the ad) before banking executives with Citibank worldwide brought a negative response regarding the overall red tone of the ad. Red in financial circles is fraught with negative associations like losses and "red ink." Nuclear Utility Services (N.U.S.), a consulting firm to the nuclear industry, insisted that all their photography emphasize the color blue, which invokes a sense of security and safety, and minimize or eliminate any use of the colors red or yellow which signify danger or caution.

COLOR ASSOCIATIONS

Red/Red-Orange

danger	heat	blood	friction	irritation
evil	Satanism	love	fire	war
fury	disgust	appetite	strength	excitement
sexuality	impulsiveness	extroversion	over-stimulation	passion
domination	rebellion	energy	arousal	confidence
	anger	rage	torment	

Yellow

heat	light	holiness	goodness	newness
cowardice	caution	wholesomeness	sun	warning
cheeriness	brightness	radiance	stimulation	warmth
openness	freedom	purity	serenity	comfort
hope	optimism	energy	liberation	spaciousness
change	salvation	understanding	knowledge	truth

Grayish or Greenish Yellow

envy	betrayal	falseness	doubt	distrust
harshness	pollution	sickly	unhealthy	repellent
		alien		

Green

growth	fertility	renewal	vitality	static energy
potential	passivity	stability	solidity	constancy
persistence	resilience	contentment	tranquillity	jealousy
	money		Irish	

Yellowish Green

hope	youth	optimism	joy

Grayish Green

mold	death	decay	rot	sickness

Bluish Green

cold	vigor	aggression	firmness

Blue

calming	restful	serene	cool/cold	peace
gentleness	refreshment	satisfaction	contentment	loyalty
trust	devotion	eternity	harmony	motherly love
passivity	introversion	sky	space	distance
water	winter	immortality (Chinese)	ice	shadow
	boy		baby (pastel)	

Dull/Grayish Blue

depression	fear	grief	perdition

Violet/Purple

Medium/neutral	Dark/Bluish	Light/Reddish	Light/Grayish
mysterious	ominous	spiritualism	space
regal	terrifying	enchantment	great distance
impressive	death	delicacy	
pious	solitude	divine love	

White				
purity	chastity	clarity	light	radiance
cleanliness	divinity	weightlessness	eternity	openness
freedom	medicinal	bridal	virginal	antiseptic
innocence	heavenly	death (Chinese)	clouds	snow

Gray				
restfulness	depression	lifelessness	noncommitment	gloom
dullness	neutrality	moodiness	drabness	dreariness
	unemotional	boredom	colorless	

Black				
death	emptiness	annihilation	mourning	limitless void
universe	mystery	witchcraft	superstition	evil
despair	night	demonic	the unknown	fear
	sophistication (dress)		clergy (Judeo-Christian)	

The point is that, even beyond the effect that distance has on light and color, the computer artist must use color effectively on other levels as well. He or she must be able to convincingly create a visual simulation of the effects of nature without nature's help. In order to achieve this, the artist must observe the interaction between all of nature's forces.

However, beyond simulating the reaction of the forces of nature on light and color, the artist also has the power to use the computer to affect his or her audience with the emotional triggers and symbolism associated with color. To accomplish this, a full knowledge of the meaning of color by the artist/designer is imperative.

Most artists use color intuitively which, to a large measure, is how color affects the observer or viewer. But it is even more powerful as a subconscious communication tool when it is used intentionally, intellectually, or to alter and effect mood, atmosphere, and emotion(almost to a spiritual level(associated with the image. Color has a definite physiological effect on all living things, and its emotional or psychological responses to color often seem arbitrary and personal. However, when colors are combined with the correct visual symbols and set in the proper context, the general reactions are usually predictable.

Its power is that it can move one far beyond the literal content of the image.

1

MOLSON

MR. COOL

The concept was fairly simple and straight forward. Show a "cool" looking guy (no pun intended) made of ice, rising out of a cooler. Naturally, the cooler was to be packed with Molson beer. An open bottle of Molson beer was to be held in one hand and, according to the layout, he was to be holding a volleyball in the other hand. His attire, supplied by the client, was to be a Molson volley ball T-shirt. The shirt was the promotional premium for that summer. Molson was also sponsoring volleyball tournaments around the country.

Solutions are rarely as straight forward as the problems that prompt them. Getting a model maker to create an ice figure out of Plexiglas was out of the question since the actual display was to be life sized. Plexiglas is a very expensive and difficult medium to work with. Getting it to hold the ball and the beer bottle convincingly would be a major accomplishment for both the model maker and the photographer.

Ruling out the Plexiglas ice sculpture left only one other course of action: photograph a real male model wearing the T-shirt, holding the beer (for position only) and the volleyball, then make him appear to be made of ice—an ice sculpture maintaining all the subtle detail that would make it a convincing representation of a living man. (1-1)

A block of Plexiglas ice was selected, from a model maker who specializes in Plexiglas models, for its texture, chips, and contours. How the contours of the surface of the ice caught the light was extremely important. The distortion, created by the ice, of an object seen through it was another factor to take into consideration in making the final image convincing. In this case, the Plexiglas ice was as important for reference as it was for photography. (1-2)

Another necessity was a beauty shot of the product. A shot that would open up the dark brown-looking bottle with light to give it life, creating an inviting aura of freshness and refreshment. This would be extremely difficult to achieve while the bottle was in the model's hand. The bottle had to be shot at the same angle as the one the model was holding since it was going to replace the bottle in the original shot. (1-3)

The same challenges and goals applied to shooting the cooler chest that was to appear full of ice and product. It was filled half way with plexi-crushed ice that was rented from a model maker. Buried under the "ice" were two strobe heads to light it from below and open it up. Each bottle had a reflector behind it to send more light through and open it up. (1-4)

Once the photography is completed, and the selected images are digitized and converted to images the computer can understand, the next creative process begins with the computer and the image editing software. The first step in the challenging process of turning our flesh and blood model into one of "ice and water" was to silhouette him. There are several ways to isolate an object. When it's possible to control the color of the background surrounding the object, silhouetting becomes almost automatic. To silhouette an object based on color, use the chrome key masking function. Select the color that is to be masked along with every part or selected

1-2

1-3

1-1

1-4

area of the image containing the selected color; only that color will be masked. The most important point is to be sure that the color of the background is not contained in the object to be silhouetted. Specifically near or on the edge of the object because the chrome key masking function will not be able to distinguish between the background and its edge. This is a particularly valuable function when dealing with highly detailed edges or when hair has to be silhouetted.

Once you start working with the image, whatever imperfections are to be eliminated or fixed should be taken care of at the start. It will be more difficult to retouch after assembly or manipulation has begun. There is also a chance that it might be overlooked and forgotten after the image has been printed and it's too late to make any changes. (1-5)

Once the silhouette was accomplished, the next step was to enlarge the area to be worked on. Since the T-shirt was not going to be manipulated, I was able to work on the head and arms separately. I made a separate canvas of the original head and neck before I started for two reasons. The first was to enable me to restore any part of the original face that I may want to restore later, or even to start over if I wanted to try a different approach. There is no right or wrong way to create any effect, and if one approach doesn't work, it is comforting to know one can exercise other options by having the original image available. The second is that there are details in the face and hands that

have to be reincorporated back into the image. (1-6)

After the head and neck were enlarged, I picked up the block of ice in the warping tool and proceeded to push, pull, and stretch the ice over the contour of the model's face. I adapted the more textured parts of the ice block for the hair and applied them to the appropriate areas with the cloning brush and the warping tool. Highlights were added in much the same way to give the face a rough sense of volume and form. (1-7)

To create a smooth ice-like surface on the face, the smoothing or smear brush was used to even out the surface and the cloning brush was used to capture highlights and textures that seemed appropriate. The cloning brush was also needed to give the head and neck form and texture. Once that had been accomplished, the process of restoring selected details of the face was next. The mouth, ears, nose, and eyeglasses were restored in gray and white. The grays were matched to the grays found in the ice to create the illusion of the face as being a part of the ice. This was accomplished in the color correction module, partially by playing with the color correction curves. The details of the teeth were only suggested to maintain a feeling of ice and not stone sculpture. (1-8)

To give the ice man a three-dimensional and life-like quality, the eyeglasses were fully restored in color. Shadows from the glasses were added to enhance the illusion of reality so they were obviously not part of the sculpture. (1-9)

1-5

The art director felt that the glasses were too shiny and distracting. He also wanted the color to relate more to the color of the logo on the T-shirt. By using the blurring brush, I was able to eliminate the reflections in the lenses. Changing the color of only the lenses required masking by using the line art tools to outline the lenses. Then I filled the shapes with the mask. Reversing the mask was the next step. I left the lenses as the only parts of the image unmasked. This allowed me to color shift the lenses by manipulating the color curves until the color was in the magenta family and related to the hot pink of the logo without having an effect on the rest of the image. (1-10)

The next part of the figure to be converted to ice was the model's arm holding the volleyball. First, I created a duplicate canvas of the arm (to restore to). Then I had to isolate the area that had to be manipulated or affected without affecting the rest of the image. To achieve this, a mask had to be made to surround the arm. By chrome keying the flesh, a mask was created only for the arm. Since the arm was the only area that was to be worked on, I inverted the mask, thus isolating the arm and causing the ball, T-shirt, and background to be masked. (1-11)

Using the same technique for the arm that I used for the head, I grabbed the block of Plexiglas ice with the warping tool and stretched, pulled, and bent the ice until it conformed to the shape and contour of the arm. Cloning was used to add highlights and fill in areas that were too small to fill easily with the warping tool. (1-12)

Once the arm was upholstered with ice, the surface had to be smoothed and blended to give the arm the same ice-like surface quality as the head. Using the same gray to white scale created for the head, I selectively restored the details of the arm and hand. Fingernails, tendons, and muscles were, as is always the case in a visual situation, created by the illusion of highlight and shadow to indicate form. (1-13)

1-7

1-6

Now, one of the trickiest steps in creating this image, and one that had to be repeated on the other hand, was the next step in the process. In order to make this ice arm believable and interactive with the volleyball, the arm had to appear transparent. This part of the process is more illustration than photography or retouching. Picking out colors from the photographs of the block of plexi-ice and the volleyball, I created a paint palette from which to draw on for colors that would accurately match the colors in photographs that I was combining to create the ice man image. Using the skills of an illustrator, I painted in the ball over the hand and arm with the airbrush tool. I allowed for the distortion that would be caused by light being bent as it traveled through the uneven density of the ice of the arm. Once again, the details of the hand and arm were replaced over the painted in volleyball with the gray to white scale. Highlights and refractions were added to complete the effect of the arm being transparent while having form and volume. (1-14)

The hand holding the product was the final part of the model to be converted to ice. Once again, the first step was to duplicate the canvas or part of the image that was to be worked on. A mask had to be created for the hand gripping the bottle and the labels on the bottle. To create these masks, the line art capability was used to outline the areas that were to be masked. The colors in the arm, specifically the shadow areas, were too similar to the browns in the bottle for the chrome key capability to create the mask effectively. The white of the shirt and the

1-10

1-9

1-8

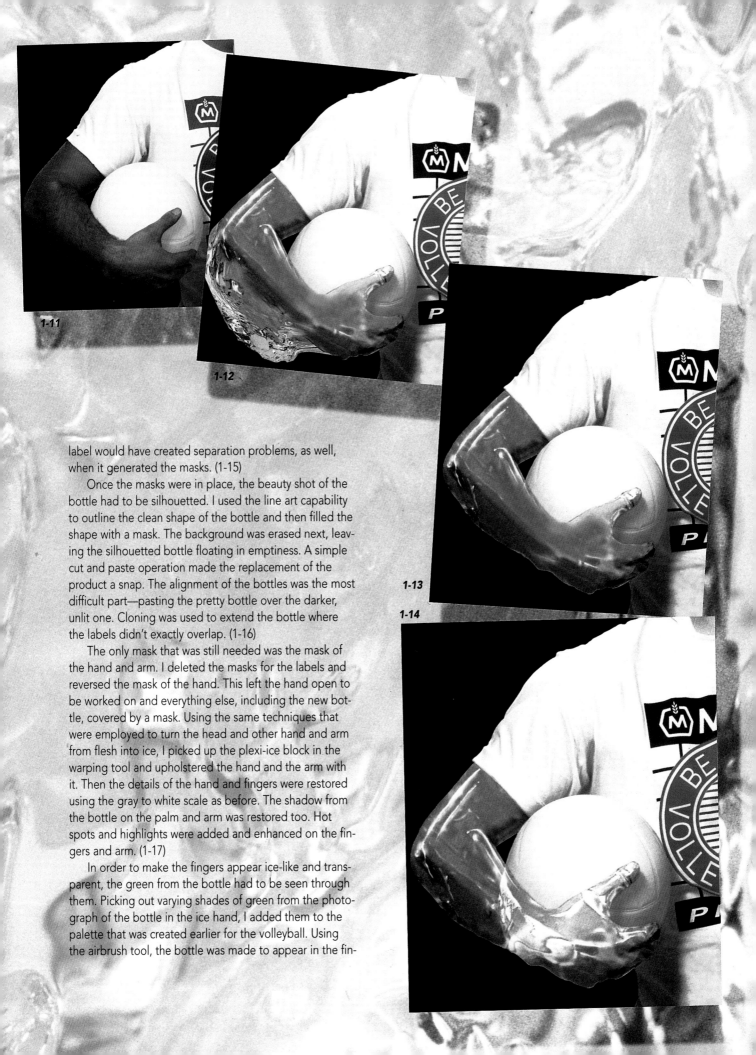

1-11

1-12

1-13

1-14

label would have created separation problems, as well, when it generated the masks. (1-15)

Once the masks were in place, the beauty shot of the bottle had to be silhouetted. I used the line art capability to outline the clean shape of the bottle and then filled the shape with a mask. The background was erased next, leaving the silhouetted bottle floating in emptiness. A simple cut and paste operation made the replacement of the product a snap. The alignment of the bottles was the most difficult part—pasting the pretty bottle over the darker, unlit one. Cloning was used to extend the bottle where the labels didn't exactly overlap. (1-16)

The only mask that was still needed was the mask of the hand and arm. I deleted the masks for the labels and reversed the mask of the hand. This left the hand open to be worked on and everything else, including the new bottle, covered by a mask. Using the same techniques that were employed to turn the head and other hand and arm from flesh into ice, I picked up the plexi-ice block in the warping tool and upholstered the hand and the arm with it. Then the details of the hand and fingers were restored using the gray to white scale as before. The shadow from the bottle on the palm and arm was restored too. Hot spots and highlights were added and enhanced on the fingers and arm. (1-17)

In order to make the fingers appear ice-like and transparent, the green from the bottle had to be seen through them. Picking out varying shades of green from the photograph of the bottle in the ice hand, I added them to the palette that was created earlier for the volleyball. Using the airbrush tool, the bottle was made to appear in the fin-

1-17

1-18

1-16

1-15

gertips adding a detail that at once made the total effect credible. (1-18)

The ice man was finished, but he still had to be added to the cooler. A canvas was created, large enough for the combination of the two elements, in the size of the finished file that would be sent for output. Already a silhouette, the ice man was ready, but the cooler had to be silhouetted and retouched. Line art was used to create the mask, and the background was erased. The cooler was pasted in position. After adjusting the size of the ice man to fit proportionally in the ice chest, he was pasted over the cooler in position. Using the cloning tool, the T-shirt was extended down into the ice, and the ice was brought into the shirt until a seamless merging of the two images had taken place. (1-19)

1-19

was that in their final form, they were to look as if they were glowing The exact perspective would be fine tuned during assembly on the computer. (2-1)

Also as requested, the type that was to appear on the backs of the chips was supplied as separate pieces of line art. It was cleaner to work with and easier to streak or blur as individual pieces apart from the chips. (2-2)

They had their model maker in California create a large field of mother boards to be, in this ad, the "mother of all mother boards." It came in pieces and had to be assembled in the studio. We shot it at the approximate angle that it was to appear. As big as it was, there were plenty of spaces that had to be filled with the computer later. (2-3)

Last to arrive were the screen grabs of the different software programs that computers using these chips would be able to run more efficiently and quickly. The delay was caused by the time it took to obtain releases and permission to use the software manufacturer's copyrighted graphic displays. (2-4)

Because the layout was so tightly cropped around the products and screen displays—in order to keep them as big as possible and the displays readable(the placement of all the objects had to be planned precisely. The layout was scanned into the computer and then each element was replaced with an accurate tracing of the real components. (2-5)

A canvas the size of the final image was opened to place the chips in position. The individual chips had to be silhouetted before they were placed in position. Utilizing the chrome key mask capability, the chips and the pins were masked and the black background was made to disappear, leaving the chips floating. Care had to be taken to insure the chips were in the right order. Each chip had a different number of pins. The paste up tool was used to position them, and the perspective correction capability was used to adjust the perspective in order to have them line up precisely as they were to appear in the ad. (2-6)

To create the effect of speed, several approaches were tried including a strobe effect. When indicating speed, the first thing that an art director or designer would sketch or ask for is a stroboscopic effect. It works very well as an illustration on a layout to convey speed, but a series of frozen images actually slows down the effect of speedy movement in a photograph. A streak or latent image trail works much better. First, a sampling of the color from the bottom part of the chip was taken to create a palette. Then, using the airbrush tool, a slightly transparent line was extended that would taper off and fade out. The process was repeated along the bottom of each chip. A slight blending across each bottom of the chips were also

2-2

2-1

2-4

2-3

2

INTEL

INTRODUCTION OF THE PENTIUM/DX2 CHIP

To introduce the Pentium chip, the next generation of high speed processors, Intel decided to show its speed relative to its two previous products. They also wanted to illustrate its power by indicating how it speeds through software application upon software application. The concept was superior speed, power, and universality. Unfortunately there were delays in the release of the Pentium chip, but in the meantime they were releasing the DX2. Since the concept was the same, they called on me to adapt the same components for the introduction of the new DX2 chip in its place. The client supplied oversized models of the i386, i486, and the Pentium chips. They also supplied screen grabs of the appropriate software, line art of the type that goes on the back of the chips, and a large model mother board that was actually comprised of several normal sized mother boards.

Ninety nine percent of the work I do, and have done for the last 25 years, is problem solving. Throughout most of my special effects career, it meant working it out in the camera with filters, special lenses, and techniques. Sometimes it was a situation that called for figuring it out in the studio with special rigging, lighting, and innovation. When that didn't work, the only alternative was hours, days, and sometimes weeks in the darkroom devising ways to overcome the limitations of the art and technology of traditional photographic methods. This is why having a graphic color workstation for the last nine years to help solve most of these challenges has been the answer to many prayers.

When the call came from the agency to do an assignment for Intel, naturally, it was received with great joy. Most of Intel's ads had consisted of a creative use of models that were photographed, then embellished on a computer. The faxed layout that followed was indeed a departure. It still involved the use of models but as components, not as the final image that needed embellishment.

Since conceptual layouts leave a lot to interpretation, such as how big a specific glow should be or how intense, we discussed in detail how the art director and the client saw the finished piece. We had to make the screen grabs dense enough to be recognizable and readable, but still able to convey the message that these are screen displays and, are therefore, made of light and are not solid objects.

The client supplied accurate oversized mockups of the Pentium, the i386, and the i486 chips without type as I had requested. They were photographed in the approximate perspective and angle that they would appear in the ad on a solid black background. This would make silhouetting the three chips easier once they were imported into the computer. Care had to be taken to illuminate the pins so that they wouldn't disappear into the background. Another consideration

Catch a rising star.

applied to create the illusion that the streaks were generated by the entire chip. (2-7)

Once the line art of the type was scanned into the computer, a variety of effects could be applied to it. First, the type had to be reversed. The next step was to silhouette the type. This was done using the automatic function of chrome key masking or masking a single color—in this case, white. The background was dropped out and the type was assembled with the Intel logo as it appeared on the backs of the smaller "real" chips. After cutting out the assembled type, a paste up brush was made and blurs (or streaks) were created with the assembled type by dragging the type across a blank canvas. (2-8)

With the help of the perspective distortion capabilities of the paste up tool, the streaked type was matched to the perspective of the line of chips already pasted in place. The type for each chip was pasted into position individually. (2-9)

An opacity mask was used to isolate the pins on each chip. The opacity mask was created to cover only the part of the canvas that contained digital information in the same opacity or transparency inherent in the masked object. It's quick, easy, and effective. Once the pins and the chips were masked, the glow was created by using the airbrush painting tool to surround the tips of all the pins with a large circular spread of red. Over the red, a medium orange circle was painted, topped by a smaller yellow circle, followed by an even smaller white circle. The farther back their location, the smaller the pins became. Naturally, the size of the airbrush was reduced as the size of the pins became smaller. (2-10)

The screen grab displays represented a different challenge: how to make the screens look like they were made of light and were not solid objects. Transparency was the

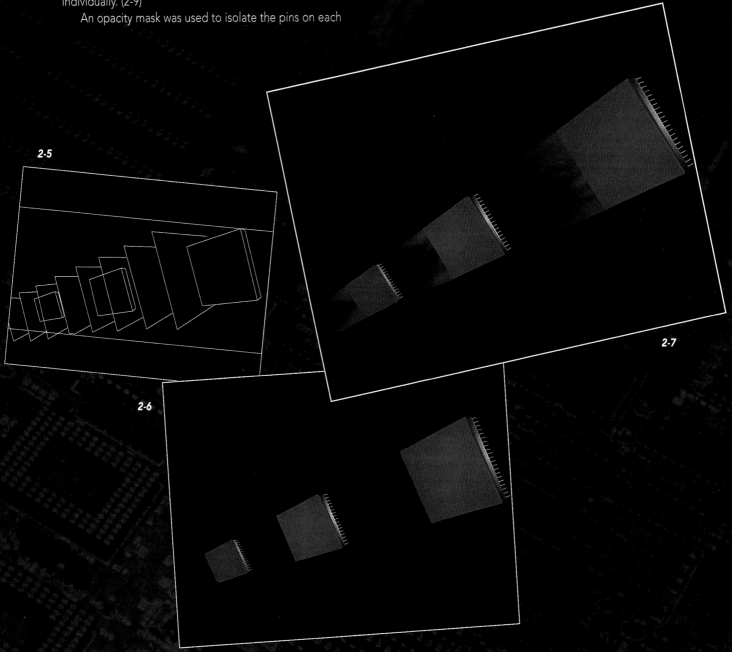

2-5

2-6

2-7

key to giving the screens a diaphanous quality. Obviously, the perspective orientation of the screens were one point perspective. The screen grabs were already silhouetted but each still required a full opaque mask for some of the effects that were to be added later. A new canvas was created on which the glowing screens were to be combined, that was identical in size to the one that contained the chip assembly. After each screen was sized, perspective distorted, and placed in position, an opaque mask was made and saved separately. Once the masks were created, the assembly began. The bottom screen was pasted in position. The next screen was pasted in its position at 50 percent opacity. On top of the second screen, the mask of the first was placed in perfect register with its screen. The second screen was then repasted over itself at 100 percent opacity with the mask of the first maintaining its 50 percent transparency. The third screen was placed so that it

did not overlap the first screen and its mask, but did overlap the second at 50 percent opacity. This was followed by the mask of the second screen pasted over the third in perfect register with its second screen. Then the third screen was repasted at 100 percent opacity over its 50 percent self. The process was then repeated over and over until all the screens were in place with a transparent, see-through screen under it. (2-11)

To indicate that the screens were made of light, we used the oldest symbol for energy, power, divination, and light: an added glow around the screen. The accumulated collection of masks that were pasted on the canvas was deleted, but the original individual masks were retained in reserve. Once again, each screen starting with the first had to be masked, but in a different combination. The first screen was masked and so was the second screen. Using

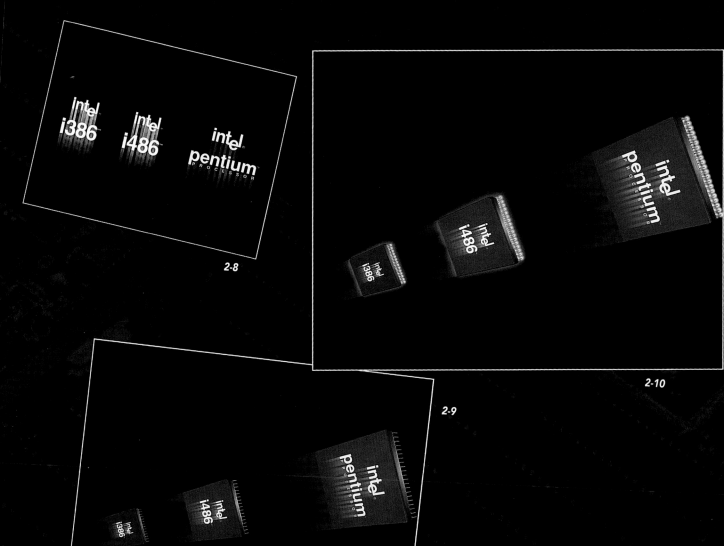

2-8

2-9

2-10

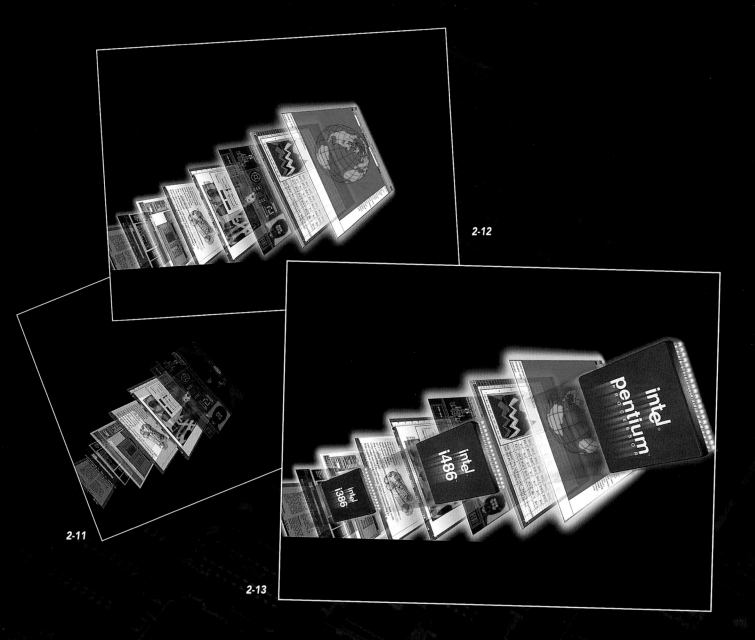

2-12

2-11

2-13

the airbrush set at 30 percent transparency, and the color, after much experimenting, was set at a variation of cyan, the glow was painted around the uncovered part of the first screen. These two masks were deleted and the same opaque mask for the first screen was placed back over the screen. The second screen's mask was then inverted so that the second mask formed a clear window around the second screen allowing the glow to be continued around the first screen at 10 percent opacity. This gave the impression that the glow was seen through the second screen. Both masks were deleted and the second screen's solid mask was repasted with the third screen's solid mask as was done with the first and second screens' masks. The same procedure was followed with each screen until they glowed. Allowing for the increase in the size of the glow as the screens came forward was important to the illusion. (2-12)

Once the glows around the screens were finished, the screens had to be deleted. The three zooming chips that

were already pasted in position on another canvas were pasted over the glowing screens. (2-13)

To create the background, a new canvas that was the same size as the others was opened. The "mother of all mother boards" did not fill the canvas when it was reduced to the proportional size needed to give it a landscape quality as seen from an aerial view. To fill in the spaces that were left, a combination of cut-and-paste and cloning were utilized. For the larger spaces, sections were cut out and altered with the perspective correction capability to match the area surrounding the hole to be filled. The altered section was then pasted into position. Smaller areas, or areas that were in need of modification, were corrected with the cloning tool. (2-14)

Unfortunately, the color of the board was monochromatic and dull brown, which matched the chips. The color had to be more interesting. First, we played with the curves in the color correction capabilities to color shift the

board to a blue/magenta color. This created a night light effect. A second duplicate canvas was created and the blue board was pasted on the second canvas. This second version was made much darker by manipulating the curves in the color correction module but still retained some detail. To add drama to the electronic landscape and increase the sense of expanse that the art director and I felt it necessary to invoke, we decided to grade the top of the image to almost black. This would give the impression that the foreground was illuminated by the glowing screens and chips. This effect was achieved by creating a graded mask that went from a 100 percent opacity at the bottom of the canvas to zero percent opacity at the top over the lighter blue/magenta landscape. The darker landscape was pasted over it resulting in a gradated landscape from light to dark. (2-15)

The final step was to paste the combined canvases of the chips and the screens over the gradated landscape. (2-16)

The same techiques and most of the same components were used to create the new image for the i486/DX2.

2-14

2-15

2-16

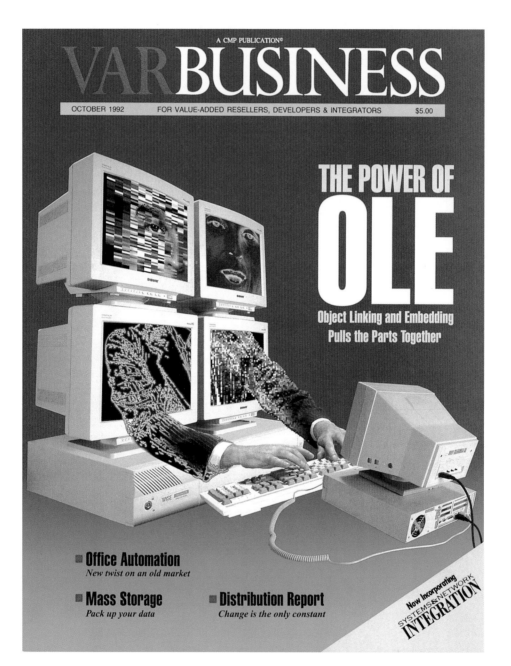

A CMP PUBLICATION®

VARBUSINESS

OCTOBER 1992   FOR VALUE-ADDED RESELLERS, DEVELOPERS & INTEGRATORS $5.00

THE POWER OF
OLE
Object Linking and Embedding
Pulls the Parts Together

■ **Office Automation**
New twist on an old market

■ **Mass Storage**
Pack up your data

■ **Distribution Report**
Change is the only constant

Now Incorporating
SYSTEMS & NETWORK
INTEGRATION

3

VAR BUSINESS MAGAZINE

"THE POWER OF O.L.E." COVER

The cover idea was to illustrate one or more computers telling other computers what to do without human intervention. That concept has been the plot line for a myriad of science fiction stories. From a revolt of machines against man to a story about a Utopian society run by machines for their human masters, science fiction and high technology has always made for intriguing story telling. When the fiction becomes fact, it also becomes a concept for a cover story to appear in magazines like *Var Business*. The art director wanted to show direct control between the master computer and the slave computer. He also wanted some kind of symbolic indication that there were several independent tasks, "multi-tasking," being communicated to the slave computer. This was visualized by ganging up four computer monitors and treating images with a different electronic pattern in each screen. It was also decided to have separate faces in two of the monitors to emphasize that each were tasks independent of the others. To indicate independent control, the arms reached out to the keyboard of the slave computer from different monitors.

Because the hands were small and both the arms and the face were going to be manipulated electronically, it was decided to use an executive looking member of the editorial staff as the model. It also represented a significant savings to a tight editorial budget in the form of model fees.

The arm and hand shot was done with the slave computer's keyboard. This gave the arms a realistic reach and proportion. It also enabled the model to pose in a relaxed way, allowing a natural interaction with the keyboard. When the shoot was over, we made marks of the keyboard's position so that we would know where to place the slave computer. (3-1)

The model's face was shot with his mouth open as if he was talking to represent the audio part of the multimedia tasking that was possible. Only one shot was made to work for the two faces, saving the cost of an additional scan. The shot was simply cropped two different ways. (3-2)

Using the Polaroids from the shoot of the male model, we constructed a set up with four monitors. They were shot with a wide angle lens to exaggerate the height, add drama, and indicate power and dominance. To make my life easier, the monitors were precariously balanced with supporting blocks that were hidden to make their silhouetting easier. A line was drawn parallel to the front of the computer monitors to indicate where the processor should be placed to be photographed. (3-3)

The slave PC was set up relative to the marks that were made around the keyboard, and the camera was still in the same position as it was for the arms. This made for consistency in the perspective, the sizing, and the lighting of the slave PC. (3-4)

Using the marks drawn when the computer monitors were shot, the processor was placed carefully behind the line. The camera position hadn't changed after the shot of the monitors and the arms were finished. However, to duplicate the angle of view, the camera had to be raised to compensate for the height of the processor since the monitors were sitting on the same surface that the processor was sitting on. (3-5)

Each of the monitors had to be silhouetted, including the screen area. The line art method of silhouetting was used to create the shape that was filled with a mask. Once the mask was in place, line art silhouettes of the screens were made and filled using the mask erase mode, which emptied the screen shapes of mask. The canvas was cleared, which meant that everything that wasn't masked was erased(including the background. A larger canvas was created, and the monitors were pasted down. (3-6)

To silhouette the arms and keyboard, I used the chrome key masking capability for the man and finished the hands and keyboard with line art masking. Once the background had been erased, the arms and torso were ready to be pasted into position. A duplicate canvas of the monitors was created as a source from which to restore the original monitor image. The arms, torso, and keyboard were pasted into position over the monitors. (3-7)

Using the restore paint capability, the original monitors were picked up from the duplicate canvas and painted through the shoulders, chest, and around the arms to create the illusion of the arms coming out of the screens. (3-8)

The model's face was cropped two ways for placement into the two top screens. Although the same face was used for both screens, the treatment was different for each. This symbolic treatment communicated that the same computer was overseeing different tasks. By cropping the same face differently(one featuring just the eye and the other featuring both eyes and the mouth(it was hoped that it would appear one task was more routine and the other would represent the audio-visual capabilities of computers. The screen closest to the reader would contain the single eye, and it would be pixellated, a more common and recognized computer digital pattern, to represent the more common computer tasks. To create the image on the screen, two identical canvases were created with the same image on both of them. One of the canvases was digitized.

To explain the process, the individual pixels (infinitesimal squares that have a single flat color) are the blocks that make up the image. These act as dots in a halftone screen and are so small they are virtually invisible to the eye. Instead, they blend together to form a smooth tonality that forms the gradated tones of a continuous tone photographic image. Through the software program that creates a pixellated pattern, blocks of pixels are brought together to form a single visible block that contains a single color, which is the average of the group of pixels in that block. These larger blocks form the same image but now the block or simulated pixel pattern is visible. If a larger block pattern is desired, more blocks are grouped and averaged into a courser block patterned image.

For the eye, a very bold pixellated pattern was decided on. However, the eye became obscured by the block pattern. Rather than play with sub-tleties of smaller blocks or a combination of large and small blocks, it was decided to restore the original photographic eye from the duplicate canvas and merge it with the pixellated patterned image for a faster read. (3-9)

The second cropping of the face, containing both the eyes and the mouth, was meant to symbolize the more recent development in audio and

3-1

3-2

3-3

3-4

3-5

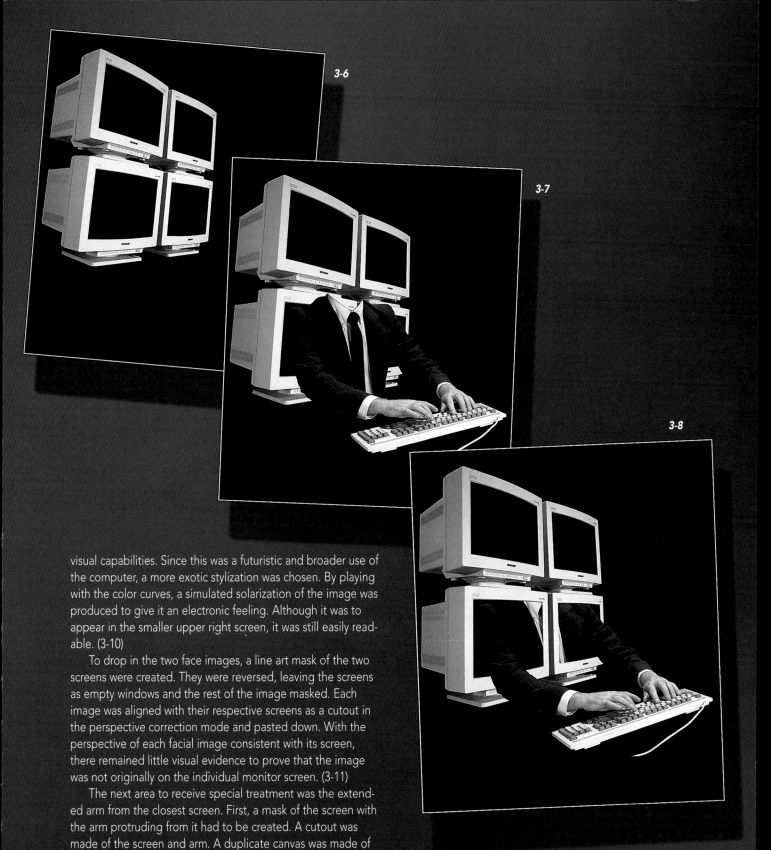

3-6

3-7

3-8

visual capabilities. Since this was a futuristic and broader use of the computer, a more exotic stylization was chosen. By playing with the color curves, a simulated solarization of the image was produced to give it an electronic feeling. Although it was to appear in the smaller upper right screen, it was still easily readable. (3-10)

To drop in the two face images, a line art mask of the two screens were created. They were reversed, leaving the screens as empty windows and the rest of the image masked. Each image was aligned with their respective screens as a cutout in the perspective correction mode and pasted down. With the perspective of each facial image consistent with its screen, there remained little visual evidence to prove that the image was not originally on the individual monitor screen. (3-11)

The next area to receive special treatment was the extended arm from the closest screen. First, a mask of the screen with the arm protruding from it had to be created. A cutout was made of the screen and arm. A duplicate canvas was made of the cutout from which to restore. After trying several different techniques, it was decided that a linear conversion in the two dominant colors of the diagonally opposite screen would give the arm a high-tech look and also tie the four screens into a unit. The mask was reversed and another canvas of the screen and arm was made. This second canvas was turned into a high contrast version. Using the ability of the computer to turn a

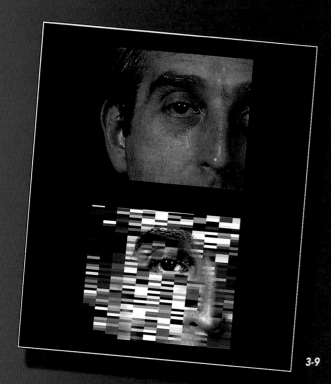

3-9

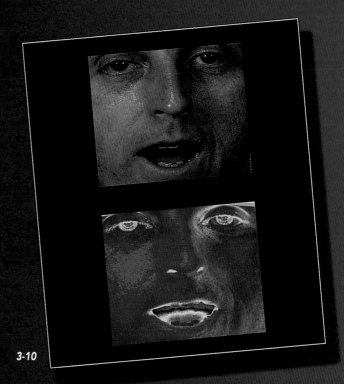

3-10

continuous tone image into line art by translating the border of contrasting tones into a line, the image of the torso and arm were turned into glowing lines.

To accomplish the transformation of the line art version of the chest inside the screen and the arm into glowing lines, the line art was used like railroad tracks for the air brush paint tool. The first trip around the line art "railway" was with a medium-sized red airbrush. The second pass was with a slightly smaller orange brush, followed by a

third pass with a small yellow airbrush. The effect was an arm and chest that looked like they were made out of neon tubing.

However, we wanted to keep the hands on the keyboard looking human because the slave computer was reacting as if a human being was controlling it. To that end, the restore function was used with a large airbrush to repaint in the natural hand and blend it with the neon arm. (3-12)

3-11

3-12

3-13

The other arm needed an equal but different treatment. It had to have the same visual weight to balance the first. To tie the four screens together as a visual unit, this chest and arm had to pick up most of the colors from the diagonally opposite screen that featured the eye. A different pixellation of the arm/hand/chest image was chosen for the second arm. It would also tie it in with the upper screen in a general way.

As was done with the other arm, the mask was reversed and a duplicate chest/arm/hand image was made. The duplicate was lightened by playing with the curves in the color correction module until more tonal detail in the model's dark brown suit was visible. Contrast was then increased until a good separation of tonal planes and areas was achieved. The color curves were manipulated individually to bring out different colors. Finally, the image was pixellated(turned into tiny squares of color(until the desired texture was achieved. To restore the natural

3-14

hand and the lower arm, the largest sized airbrush was used to paint it back into the pixellated image. (3-13)

The completed combination of manipulated and natural hands/arms/chest were pasted into their respective screens and the wire attached to the keyboard was removed. (3-14)

The next element to be added to this construction of individual pieces was the processor that supports the four screens. In the line art mode, the processor was outlined and the shape filled with mask. The surrounding image was then deleted.

An opacity mask was created over the assembled image(the four monitors with the hands on the keyboard. The opacity mask is a mask that can be created only where digital information already exists on the canvas.

Since the processor was photographed in the correct perspective, once the opacity mask was in place, it only had to be sized and pasted into position. (3-15)

The smaller slave PC and its connecting wire were outlined, masked, and silhouetted in the line art mode. The power cord, labels, and other extraneous details on the back of the computer were removed with a cloning brush. This was accomplished by selecting clear areas of the back of the PC and transferring it through a paintbrush over the details scheduled for elimination. The elimination of

unwanted details can be done before assembly, after assembly, or anytime an area in need of retouching is noticed. If it isn't taken care of shortly, there is a very good chance it will be forgotten and not noticed again until it is too late to make changes. The PC, too, was shot in a perspective and lighting consistent with the rest of the objects. Once it was silhouetted and retouched it was pasted in position. (3-16)

Finally, a background was added in the under mode that went from almost black at the top of the canvas to make a white drop out of the mast and headlines stand out, gradating downward to a lighter blue green at the bottom. (3-17)

3-16

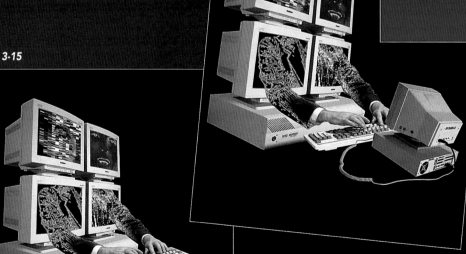

3-15

3-17

40

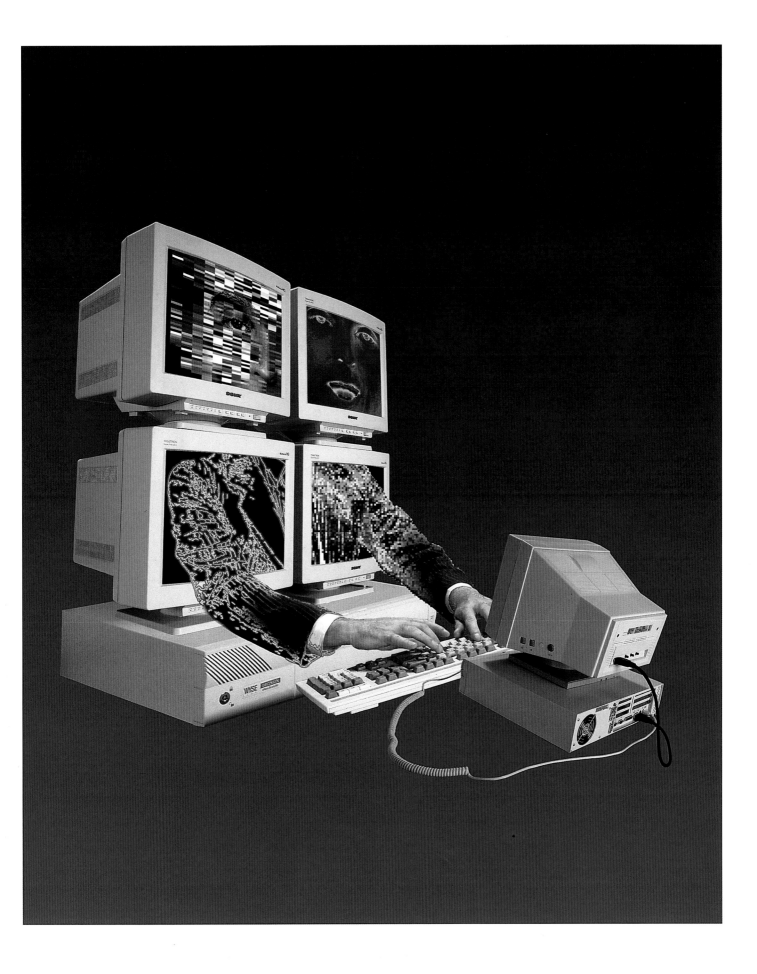

ARTHUR ASHE'S ANGUISH
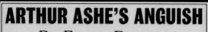
BY FRANK DEFORD

Newsweek

April 20, 1992 : $2.95

The Brain

Science Opens New Windows on the Mind

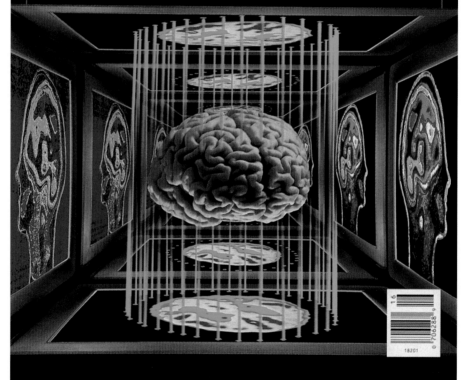

4

NEWSWEEK MAGAZINE

"THE BRAIN" COVER

The cover story concept was the future of brain research—where it was going, what fantastic breakthroughs have happened, and where they would lead. They had already ordered stock photos of MRIs, PET scans, and CAT scans, but they had no clear idea how they might use them on the cover. The assignment, as was the custom, was one of several given out to other artists and photographers for the same cover. From the five or so submissions the final cover would be selected by the editors and the publisher. Because the magazine was a news weekly, there was very little time for concepting or execution—usually three days. Even when your cover image was selected, it could be bumped for a late breaking news story. For special issues like this one, I had a little longer for concept, photography, and execution. I had less than two weeks from phone call to a finished delivered transparency.

With so little time, the art director and I discussed concepts over the phone, faxed sketches back and forth, and narrowed the possibilities that would most likely be considered. Finally two ideas, and a variation on one of them were submitted. The image that is being discussed here is the one that appeared on the cover.

It was to be a hall of giant monitors that went back to what appeared to be infinity, symbolizing unending research and the future. On the monitor screens were representations of what symbolized the state of the art research images. Floating in the center is the human brain with some type of high tech effect to symbolize on-going research.

First, we ordered a rubber cast of a real human brain from a medical supply house in California. When it arrived, we shot it from several angles with different lighting, all of which might have worked in the final assembly. When the film came back from the lab, the one that looked most aesthetic and least like a ball of pasta was picked. (4-1)

Several Magnetic Resonant Imaging (MRI) chromes were sent by the magazine. For this image, aesthetics, color, and pattern were the deciding factors in determining which one was chosen . (4-2)

The magazine also sent several Positron-Emission Tomography (PET) scans which were acquired from a stock photo agency. The two that were picked appeared to be variations of the same head. (4-3)

In both cases, the MRI and the PET scans, the overriding consideration was not content but symbolism and design.

A photograph of a monitor was necessary because almost all the viewing of the brain first appears there. The images are later turned into film for further study. It is also a visual symbol for the computer, without which most of the research in the article would be nonexistent. As an icon, a monitor was a must. (4-4)

To avoid the distraction of product identification, just the frame around the monitor screen was

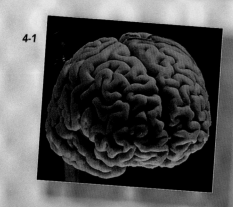

4-1

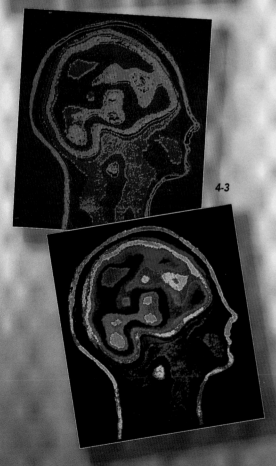

4-2

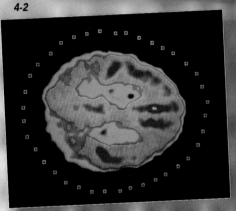

4-3

4-4

used. It alone was a very suitable icon to represent the computer and a much better graphic shape to work with. Using the line art capability, the inside edge and the outside edge of the frame were outlined. The space between was filled with mask, and the part of the image that wasn't covered by the mask was deleted. The frame itself was saved as a separate file to be used over again. A canvas the size of the monitor frame was created and the frame and its mask were pasted onto it. The green and red PET scan was then flopped and pasted inside the frame to create the left wall component. (4-5)

A new canvas identical to the first was created, and the frame with its mask were pasted onto this one. The blue PET scan was pasted inside the frame for the creation of the right wall component. (4-6)

Another canvas identical to the first two was created, and the frame and its mask were once again pasted onto it. The MRI was pasted inside this frame. This image and a duplicate mirror version were the ceiling and the floor components. (4-7)

The brain had to be silhouetted and retouched. When it arrived, there were imperfections and extraneous pieces that were left over from the mold. Since this was a model made for medical instruction and not for photography, veins and arteries had been added with what looked like a marker. All of these had to be removed before the image would be usable. The retouching was accomplished with the cloning brush by picking up good areas and painting them over the areas that needed to be improved. To silhouette the brain, the line art technique was chosen over the chrome key method because the outline is usually cleaner. However, it did involve a lot more hand work. Once the mask was in place the background was deleted. (4-8)

Ready to start the assembly, I created another canvas. This time it was the size of the final image. Its proportions were the same as it was to be on the cover, but the actual size of the image had to fit on an 8x10 inch transparency. Using the line art capability as an overlay, lines were drawn to simulate one point perspective. These lines were not a permanent part of the image, but strictly a guide for the placement of the screens. (4-9)

Once the guide lines were drawn, each screen was pasted in place forming the walls, ceiling, and floor using the perspective distortion capability. The perspective distortion capability made it possible to reshape a cut out to follow true one- or two-point perspectives. This formed the basic unit for the hall. (4-10)

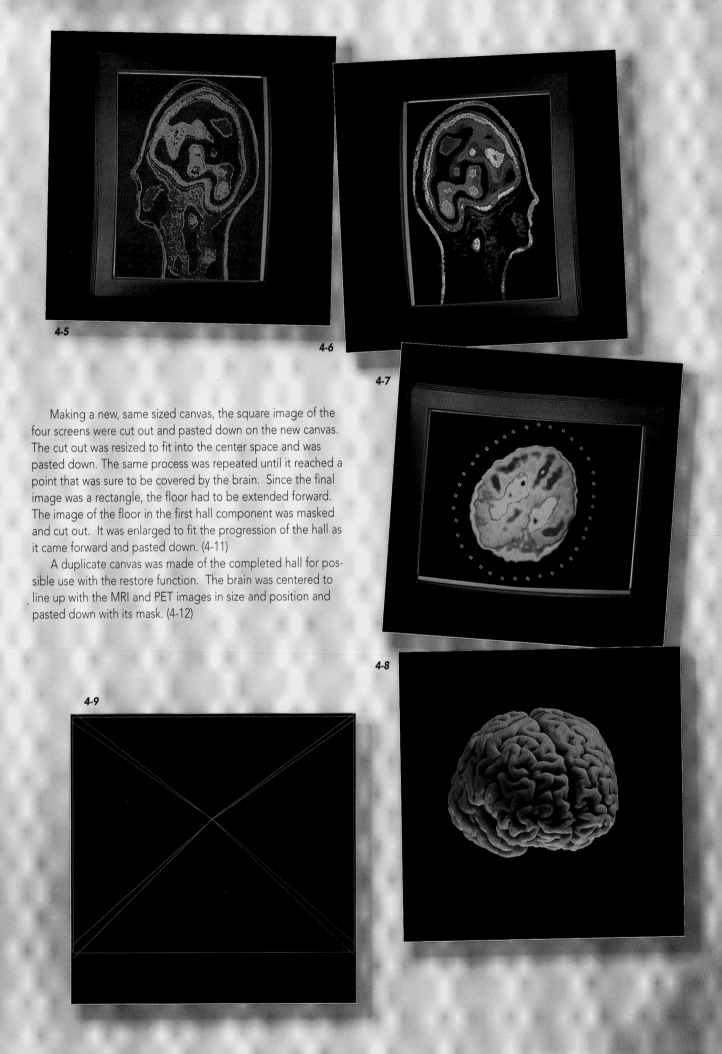

4-5

4-6

4-7

Making a new, same sized canvas, the square image of the four screens were cut out and pasted down on the new canvas. The cut out was resized to fit into the center space and was pasted down. The same process was repeated until it reached a point that was sure to be covered by the brain. Since the final image was a rectangle, the floor had to be extended forward. The image of the floor in the first hall component was masked and cut out. It was enlarged to fit the progression of the hall as it came forward and pasted down. (4-11)

A duplicate canvas was made of the completed hall for possible use with the restore function. The brain was centered to line up with the MRI and PET images in size and position and pasted down with its mask. (4-12)

4-8

4-9

4-10

4-11

4-12

To symbolize the high tech research that was going on, several techniques were tried and rejected including glows, lightning, and posterization. A more conservative approach was finally decided upon: laser beams that connected the points that circled the upper and lower MRI images. They were drawn with the airbrush in a line from top to bottom that would not be so big as to obscure the brain. The back row was drawn first with the brain mask turned on. To give the lines a glow-like feeling, two lines were drawn with the airbrush tool. The first was slightly wider and somewhat transparent. The second line was a very intense narrow line that represented the source of the glow. (4-13)

To complete the image, another duplicate canvas was made of the image with the back row drawn in. The brain mask was turned off and the rest of the laser beam lines were drawn over the brain with a more transparent airbrush. Although the brain was visible, it was obscured by the glowing blue lines. Going to the restore function and using the previous canvas, the brain was painted back in with a large transparent airbrush so as to not totally eliminate the lines and the image was in its final form.

4-13

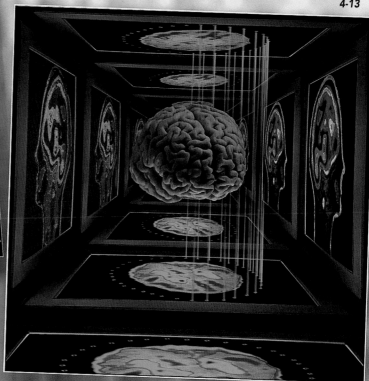

5-1

5-2

the line art module with the Bessier curves. To make the shadow red, I used the hue, value, and saturation controls to darken the red appropriately. That, too, was filled in. A chrome key mask was made of the background or shadow red shape. The two masks were saved separately. (5-5)

Again using the line art capability, three panels were drawn for the front of the umbrella, and each one was filled with mask. Each panel mask was reversed to create a window. Using the airbrush in the paint mode and a palette made from different values of the red color selected for the parachute's umbrella, highlights and shadows were painted in each panel to give it form and volume. Care had to be taken to make sure that the lighting on the umbrella, as indicated by the highlights and shadows, was

The next step in the "fragillization" of the earth was to turn the round globe into an egg shaped globe. First, I made a same size blank canvas of the globe. In the paste up mode it possible to compress the round globe into an oval shape. Then, switching to the perspective distortion capability in paste up before the object was pasted down, I tapered the upper half of the oval slightly, which also elongated the upper end. This was corrected by gently pushing down from the top until the desired egg shape was achieved. (5-4)

To create the parachute, which was all illustration, an outline of the front of the parachute's umbrella was drawn in the line art module on a new blank canvas. Using the Bessier curves, it took almost no time to achieve the perfect shape. After selecting the desired shade of red from a palette of 6.8 million possible colors, the shape was filled in. A mask was created for the umbrella by filling in the same line art shape with mask. The visible part of the rear of the umbrella was drawn in the same way by using

5-3

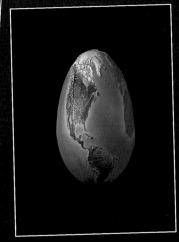

5-4

5

DISCOVER MAGAZINE

"OUR FRAGILE EARTH" COVER

The concept was not unusual; it was the fragility of the earth's ecology and all the problems that are confronting those who are trying to preserve the natural balance. The fact that the earth is in trouble is not news. How to express it in a unique way was the challenge. An egg shaped earth represented its fragility. Thousands of nails represented the constant threats to all the life forms on this earth and to the quality of life for mankind. A parachute symbolized the fact that what had been done has slowed our descent but is not enough to stop the inevitable destruction of life on this planet as we know it. The red color, signifying danger, was used for the parachute.

The impact of the computer on the industry is being felt across the board. Not only are the photographers, illustrators, and traditional retouchers with their dyes, bleaches, and airbrush changing the way they work, but peripheral services to the image making process like the model makers are very much in danger of becoming extinct. The photograph of the earth was made of a rented detailed topographic globe. It was the normal round familiar globe. At a time before computers, a model maker would have been commissioned to make an egg shaped globe, accurately detailed, and oversized. It would have required weeks of work and would have been prohibitively expensive in this climate of shrinking budgets. Instead, the reshaping was done on the computer. (5-1)

Who do you get to hammer a thousand nails into a board in a specific shape that would work perfectly with the other objects in the image? A person with a lot of patience and time on his hands. The other alternative is to have your assistant hammer about 50 nails into a piece of foamcore and take a photograph of that. The rest of the nails and the shaping would be done later. (5-2)

The red parachute isn't shown here because it was created in the computer. More and more often, objects such as the parachute and even the globe will be created in a 3D program, which is like sculpting or building an object in the computer that, when finished, will look like a photograph. It would have all the properties of an object that actually exists: it could be lit with studio-like lighting, it could be rotated and seen from any angle, and the computer could simulate a photograph of the object taken with a variety of lenses from a fisheye to a long telephoto lens.

First, the photograph of the globe had to be cleaned up with cloning since there are always imperfections that show up and must be corrected. Once the image had been made as perfect as possible, the image was silhouetted. The easiest and fastest way to create a mask for the globe was to chrome key the background and then reverse the mask. (5-3)

THE ENVIRONMENTAL DILEMMA

DISCOVER

THE WORLD OF SCIENCE

APRIL 1990
$2.95

SPECIAL ISSUE

THE STRUGGLE TO SAVE OUR PLANET

PLUS:
Touchy Robots
Raindrop Physics
Sexual Perception

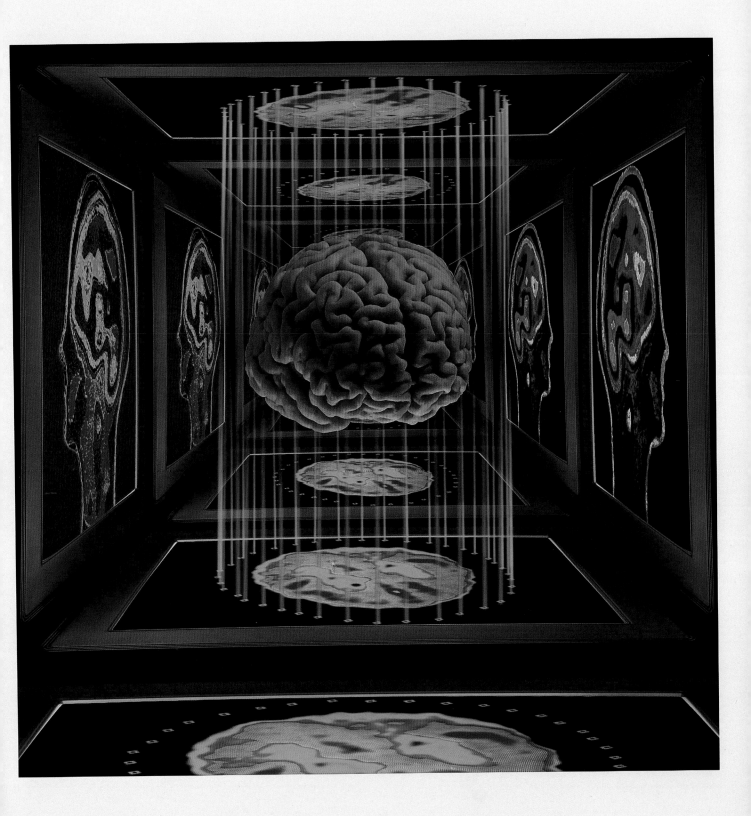

consistent with the lighting on the egg shaped earth. A similar process was repeated for the back of the umbrella. Once the painting was finished and the umbrella had a dimensional quality about it, it was ready to be joined with the egg shaped earth. (5-6)

A new canvas was created that was big enough to accommodate the egg shaped earth and the umbrella. The umbrella and the earth were pasted into position relative to each other. Using the line art module, the lines connecting the earth to the umbrella were drawn. Trial and error was the only way to determine what the correct size brush would be. If the lines were too fine they might disappear, and if the lines were too heavy they would definitely look out of proportion and be distracting. I opted

for the finest line that was reproducible to further emphasize the fragility of the earth and its tenuous situation. (5-7)

Another blank canvas was created. This time, the canvas was the size of the cover. It had to be large enough to allow for bleed because the final art was to fill the page with no borders. In the line art module, the layout was drawn that indicated the areas where the masthead and cover copy would be. The layout could be seen through the image and be turned on and off, thereby allowing it to be used as an overlay for the positioning of the various elements in the composition. In cases like this, it's absolutely necessary to avoid the kind of image and type overlaps that could cause visual confusion or difficulty in reading the type. (5-8)

5-5

5-6

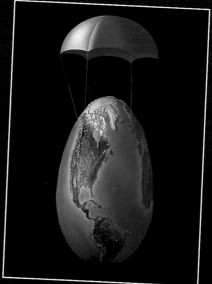

5-7

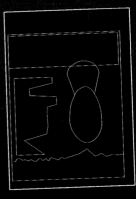

5-8

The original stand of nails was silhouetted with the chrome key masking capability, and the background was deleted. The nails were pasted down in the under mode several times in different sizes, one under the other. Each paste down was slightly smaller and darker than the previous one. (5-9)

This gave the impression that there were row upon row of nails going off into infinity as they reduced in size and faded out of sight. Cloning or transferring part of the image to another with the cloning brush in the under mode allowed for creating an interesting sky line with the tops of the nails and making a bunch of them rise to form a point directly under where the earth would be placed. (5-10)

A gradated background that went from black to dark blue was dropped behind the nails and was dark enough to allow for the type to be dropped out in yellow or white. (5-11)

Finally, the egg shaped earth with its parachute was dropped into position and pasted down to complete the image. (5-12)

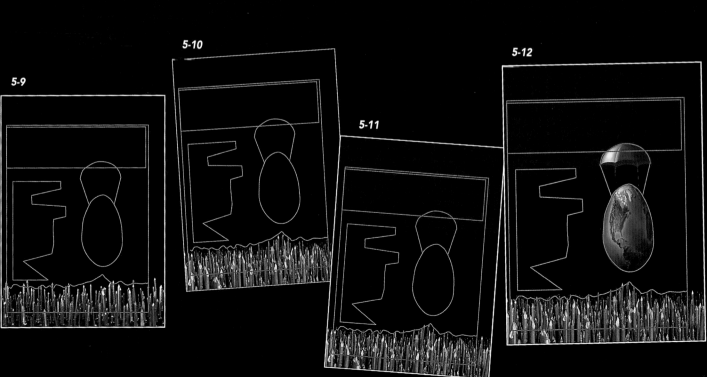

5-9

5-10

5-11

5-12

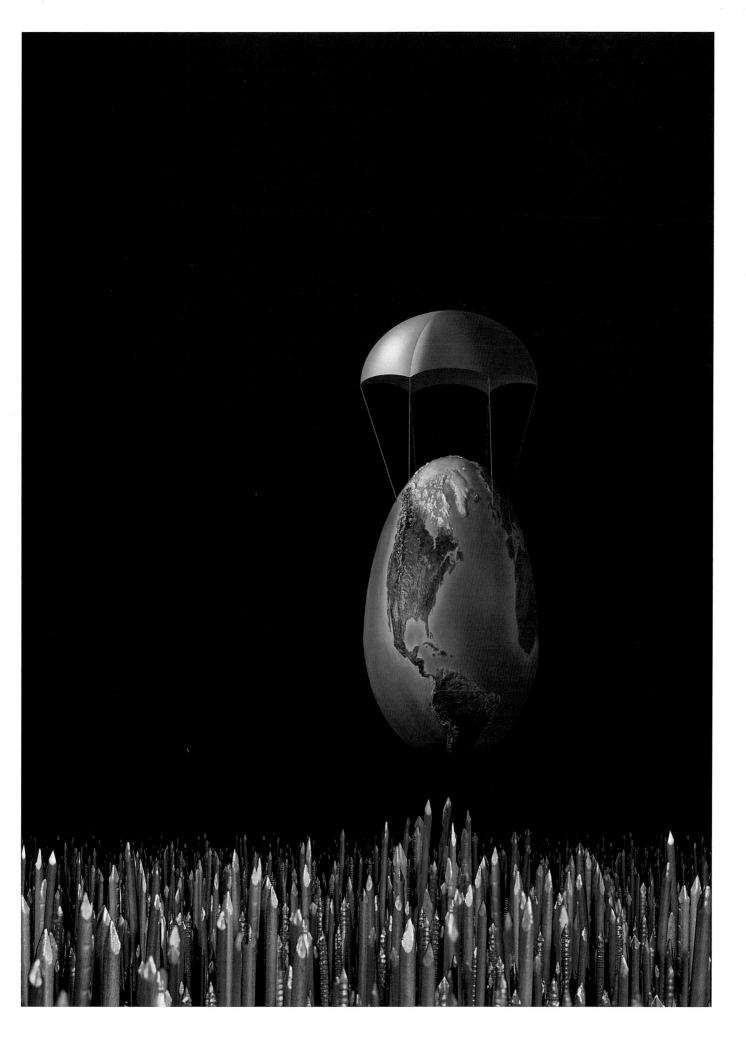

ITALY'S TESTING TIME
A Country Ripe for Reform

Newsweek.

THE INTERNATIONAL NEWSMAGAZINE

April 6, 1992

DIGITAL WIZARDS

The coming revolution in consumer electronics will change how you live and work

6

NEWSWEEK MAGAZINE

"DIGITAL WIZARDS" COVER

Since the invention of the wheel, man has transferred his burdens to machines. In this age of computers, this transference is not only of burdens requiring physical exertion but also responsibilitiy. This has accelerated beyond the wildest expectations of most of us, directly or indirectly, into every part of our existence. *Newsweek* decided to do a cover story on how far this new technology that we created has come. This was the concept to illustrate, our creation of a new technological generation. We gave it life, of sorts, and artificial intelligence. Now we are working on the ethics and laws for it.

When the art director and I discussed ideas for the cover, we kept returning to the same idea: Michaelangelo's creation of man in the Sistine Chapel. Finding a symbol for the technology without being too specific was difficult. Eventually, it led us to general electronic circuitry as an icon for technology. It seemed to be a good solution but making it work visually was the challenge.

A hand model was selected to play both roles, the hand of Adam and the hand of God. He remarked that he couldn't believe that his career as a hand model had peaked after only two years in the business. I asked what he meant by that, and he responded, "It's all down hill after you've done God."

Because there was going to be a spark between the two fingers at the point of near contact, and it represented the "life force transfer," it should definitely be the hottest light source. A bare bulb strobe head was used to simulate the light from the spark. Umbrellas and reflectors were used for the rest of the lighting. The overhead lighting used a blue gel for drama and to help the hands relate to the background, which was to be a deep blue. One of the advantages of shooting components separately is that they can be lit and composed conveniently and easily. The lighting of one component doesn't affect the other components directly until the components are assembled. However, previsualization of every detail and nuance of the components' interaction and their effect on each other is important when working this way. Since the hand of God and Adam were to be lit by the same source and in the same way, they were shot with the same lighting set up, and with the hand model in the same position, different pose. Just the camera was moved to a different angle of view. (6-1)

To make electronic circuitry a nonliteral representation that had a genuine feel to it, I felt that real circuit boards would be a good place to start. They were photographed with front lighting and balanced with back light-ing to show all the printed circuits on both sides of the boards, and the detail of the chips, capacitors, et al on the side facing the camera. It also kept the boards-from being excessively dark and brooding. (6-2)

The arm and hand of Adam were outlined in the line art module and filled with mask. To float the silhouette of the hand and arm in an empty background, the background was erased. (6-3)

A new blank canvas of identical size was created, and the silhouetted hand was duplicated

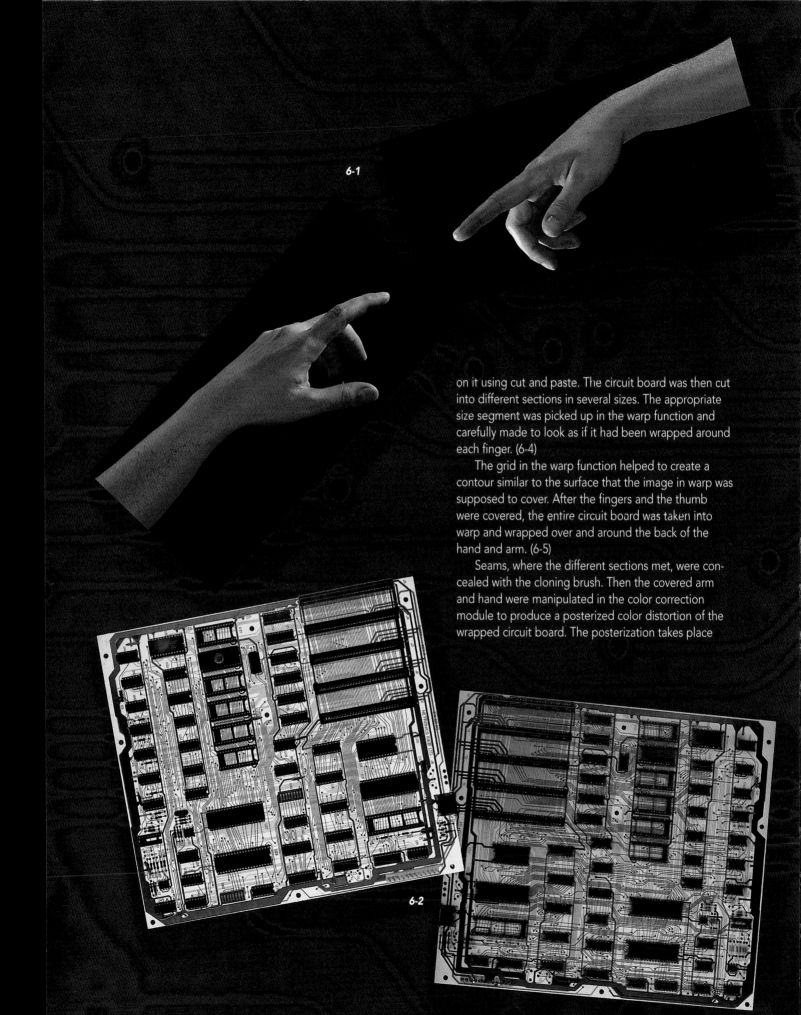

6-1

on it using cut and paste. The circuit board was then cut into different sections in several sizes. The appropriate size segment was picked up in the warp function and carefully made to look as if it had been wrapped around each finger. (6-4)

The grid in the warp function helped to create a contour similar to the surface that the image in warp was supposed to cover. After the fingers and the thumb were covered, the entire circuit board was taken into warp and wrapped over and around the back of the hand and arm. (6-5)

Seams, where the different sections met, were concealed with the cloning brush. Then the covered arm and hand were manipulated in the color correction module to produce a posterized color distortion of the wrapped circuit board. The posterization takes place

6-2

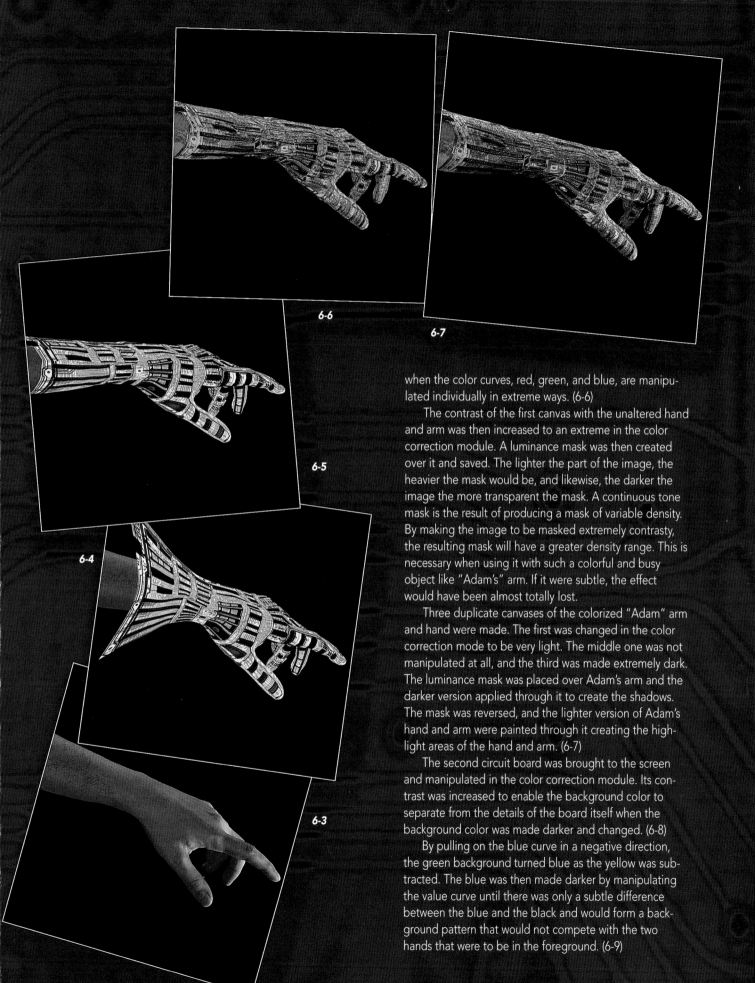

6-6

6-7

6-5

6-4

6-3

when the color curves, red, green, and blue, are manipulated individually in extreme ways. (6-6)

The contrast of the first canvas with the unaltered hand and arm was then increased to an extreme in the color correction module. A luminance mask was then created over it and saved. The lighter the part of the image, the heavier the mask would be, and likewise, the darker the image the more transparent the mask. A continuous tone mask is the result of producing a mask of variable density. By making the image to be masked extremely contrasty, the resulting mask will have a greater density range. This is necessary when using it with such a colorful and busy object like "Adam's" arm. If it were subtle, the effect would have been almost totally lost.

Three duplicate canvases of the colorized "Adam" arm and hand were made. The first was changed in the color correction mode to be very light. The middle one was not manipulated at all, and the third was made extremely dark. The luminance mask was placed over Adam's arm and the darker version applied through it to create the shadows. The mask was reversed, and the lighter version of Adam's hand and arm were painted through it creating the high-light areas of the hand and arm. (6-7)

The second circuit board was brought to the screen and manipulated in the color correction module. Its contrast was increased to enable the background color to separate from the details of the board itself when the background color was made darker and changed. (6-8)

By pulling on the blue curve in a negative direction, the green background turned blue as the yellow was sub-tracted. The blue was then made darker by manipulating the value curve until there was only a subtle difference between the blue and the black and would form a back-ground pattern that would not compete with the two hands that were to be in the foreground. (6-9)

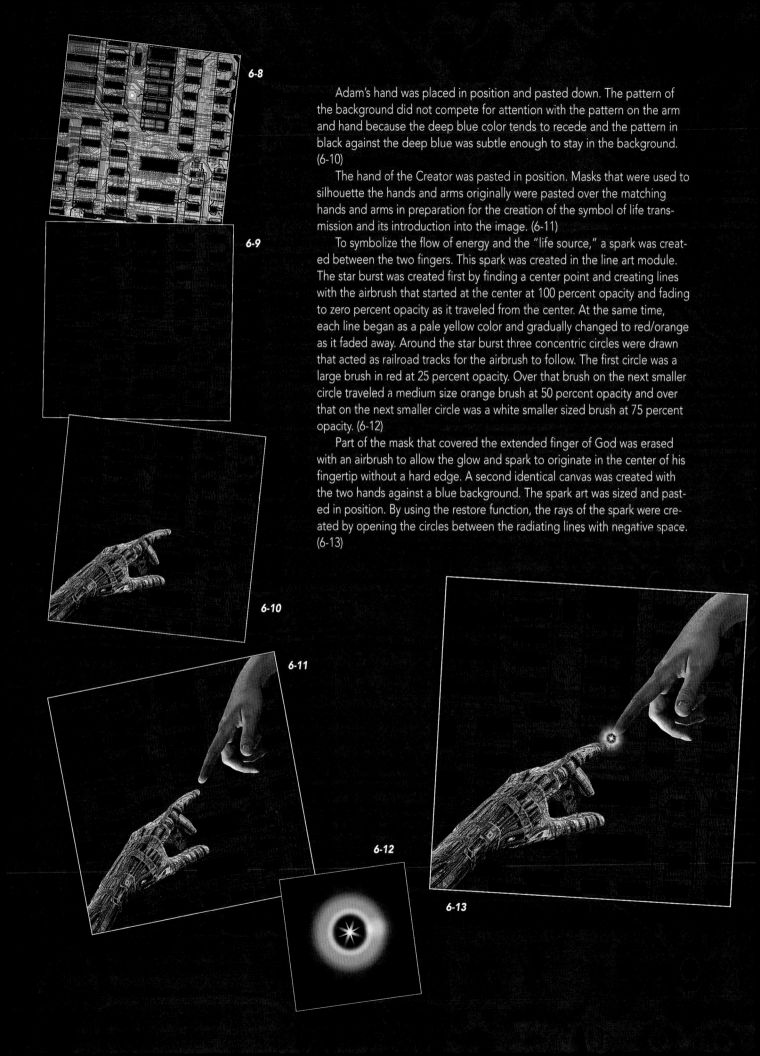

6-8

6-9

Adam's hand was placed in position and pasted down. The pattern of the background did not compete for attention with the pattern on the arm and hand because the deep blue color tends to recede and the pattern in black against the deep blue was subtle enough to stay in the background. (6-10)

The hand of the Creator was pasted in position. Masks that were used to silhouette the hands and arms originally were pasted over the matching hands and arms in preparation for the creation of the symbol of life transmission and its introduction into the image. (6-11)

To symbolize the flow of energy and the "life source," a spark was created between the two fingers. This spark was created in the line art module. The star burst was created first by finding a center point and creating lines with the airbrush that started at the center at 100 percent opacity and fading to zero percent opacity as it traveled from the center. At the same time, each line began as a pale yellow color and gradually changed to red/orange as it faded away. Around the star burst three concentric circles were drawn that acted as railroad tracks for the airbrush to follow. The first circle was a large brush in red at 25 percent opacity. Over that brush on the next smaller circle traveled a medium size orange brush at 50 percent opacity and over that on the next smaller circle was a white smaller sized brush at 75 percent opacity. (6-12)

Part of the mask that covered the extended finger of God was erased with an airbrush to allow the glow and spark to originate in the center of his fingertip without a hard edge. A second identical canvas was created with the two hands against a blue background. The spark art was sized and pasted in position. By using the restore function, the rays of the spark were created by opening the circles between the radiating lines with negative space. (6-13)

6-10

6-11

6-12

6-13

7-4

7-5

7-6

The Empire State Building part of the image was complete, and the small cut was pasted back into the full canvas. (7-11)

Next to suffer the awesome power of this east coast tsunami were two buildings, a building with a steeple and what was once the PanAm building. First, however, three small cutouts that are big enough to include the buildings were made from the waves and the city canvases. The steepled building was painted through the wave in the restore mode. (7-12)

The steeple was cut in two pieces, and the wave, painted back in through the restore function. (7-13)

A toppling steeple was created by pasting the two cutouts on an angle. (7-14)

The cloning brush was used to add falling debris and to move parts of the building to the right of center. (7-15)

To create the white water washing up against the building and the water pouring from the windows and holes in the building, the cloning brush picked up the foam and spray of the waves and were painted it into the structure. (7-16)

7-7

7-8

7-9

7-10

7-1

7-2

7-3

This image was created, for the most part, in the restore mode. By going back and forth between the city and the ocean canvases to refine the combined image on the third canvas, it was possible to achieve the highest level of perfection, wonderful subtlety, and great detail.

The wave striking the Empire State Building is a great example. Using the overlay to locate the landmark, three smaller cutouts were made, two from the ocean and one from cityscape. The building was then painted through the wave in the restore mode. (7-7)

A small cutout of the white water splash next to the building provided the white water turbulence around the base of the building. By using the warping tool to bend the splash into a curving shape, it was pasted over the base. The restore function made it possible to bring the building back through the center of the turbulence. (7-8)

Drawing from the splashing wave at the lower left through the cloning brush tool, I was able to create white water crashing against the top of the building. To make the waves wash around the front of the building, a smaller airbrush tool was used. (7-9)

The cloning tool was also used to paint the reflection at the base of the building by drawing from the reflection of the breaking wave next to it. A cut out of the middle portion of the building was made darker in the color correction module and then painted in as the shadow made by the wave. (7-10)

7

SILICON GRAPHICS

NEW YORK CITY TIDAL WAVE

The cover of a brochure promoting a virtual studio that makes the creation of impossible images possible by using Silicon Graphic workstations and equipment needs the same kind of image to make that statement for itself.

Imagine a wall of water the height of the Empire State Building sweeping over New York City for a second hit after a smaller one wiped out the smaller, weaker buildings. Imagine a photograph, not an illustration, of the cataclysmic event.

One of the advantages of being a photographer for over 20 years is having the collection of images from which to draw. Thousands of skies, waves, clouds, textures, and subjects, all of which are potential components to be used in part or as entire images, fill my files. They are all pieces that, when fit together properly, can create an incredible whole.

The best place to start a disaster scenario is with the unsuspecting victim, the city. A photograph of the Empire State Building and midtown Manhattan taken from the top of the World Trade Center came out of my files. Although it was shot in the early evening and the eventual scenario was to be midday, I wanted this shot. The signs atop several buildings were lit to add color, and brightening the cityscape overall was not going to be a problem. (7-1)

Waves are as individual as snow flakes or clouds. No matter how extensive the collection, for every use, one is more perfect than any of the others. So it was with this project. A wave from Ocean City, MD, broke just right for a wall of water about to overwhelm a stand of buildings. (7-2)

This photograph taken from an airliner between cloud layers, had the sweep and depth that an event of this magnitude required. (7-3)

Silhouetting the image of the city is the first step on this road to disaster. Because of the clean geometric shapes of the buildings, creating a line art mask was the logical method to use. (7-4)

The color correction module allowed for three major corrective procedures. The first was to lighten the cityscape as a whole, making it appear to be a midday scene. Second was to warm up the color temperature, making it a sunny day. The third was to increase the contrast to make the image snap. (7-5)

Creating a canvas proportioned to the size of the page that was to carry the image was a key step. Making two duplicate canvases was next, and pasting the wave in position on two of the three canvases followed. Next to last, and most importantly, was to trace the city in line art, position it accurately, and make it an overlay in the computer. (7-6) Using the overlay, the city was pasted accurately on the last full size canvas.

The PanAm building was cut out, then cut up, and pasted over the waves in odd angles to simulate the shattering and crumbling of the building's facade as it slams against the steeple of the building below. The top of the building was just pasted on an angle. (7-17)

Cloning was used to again paint in the water, spray, and random debris coming from the crumbling PanAm building. (7-18)

The cloning brush was also used to put a crack in the top half of the building. (7-19)

The disaster cutout on the right was completed and pasted back into the full canvas. Three new cutouts were made on the left of an area big enough to include three buildings caught in the breaking wave. (7-20)

All that would show of the building in the foreground of this rolling mass of water and foam was its top. The building was cut out of the cityscape cut and pasted on an angle in this one. (7-21)

The cloning brush carried the foam to all sides of the building. (7-22)

At the top. of the wave is the top of the RCA building painted through in the restore mode over the spray. (7-23)

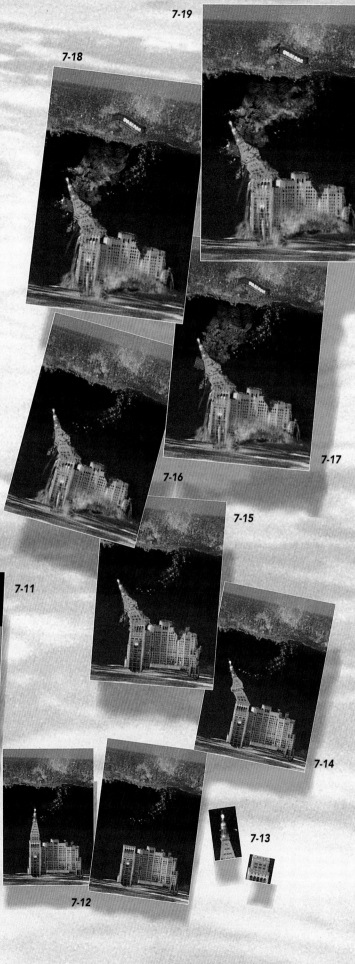

7-26

7-24

7-23

7-25

7-22

7-21

7-27

7-20

The rest of the building was cut out of the cityscape cutout, darkened in the color correction module to place it in shadow, and pasted with the warping tool after twisting and stretching part of the building to simulate a collapsing structure. (7-24)

Cloning added spray and debris to the lower structure and spray to the upper structure, firmly settling the top of the building into the wave. (7-25)

Another building was cut out of the city, and after being distorted by the warping tool it was pasted over the pounding white water. (7-26)

Once again cloning the foam, spray, and their reflection in the foreground water completed the demolition of the third building by the crashing surf. (7-27)

The finished cut was pasted back into the composition. (7-28)

To show the aftermath of the first tidal wave as the water is being drawn up into this mother of all tidal waves, three new canvases

7-28

A palette was created from the lights and darks of the building, and those colors were used to paint in interior walls and girders sticking up like blades of grass. (7-31)

The water pouring out of windows and broken walls was put there with a cloning brush. (7-32)

A duplicate cut was made of the foreground surf with the destroyed buildings and made dark with the color correction capability.

7-29

were cut from the wave and the cityscape canvases. The starting image was the swirling foam. (7-29)

Several smaller buildings were painted through the surf in the restore mode. (7-30)

Using the restore mode in reverse, the foam was painted back up to the buildings to set them into the surf. Parts of the buildings were eliminated by painting the surf over them.

7-30

7-31

7-32

7-33

7-34

7-35

7-36

7-37

This darker version was used through the restore function to paint in shadows to give the foreground buildings a sense of substance and place. (7-33)

The foreground cutout having been completed was also pasted back into the final composition. (7-34)

One last step, albeit a subtle one, remained: to place the submerged remainder of the city under water. A double cutout of the area to be worked with was made, one from the city and one from the ocean. The ocean was the basic canvas. (7-35)

Using a large airbrush with the transparency turned up in the restore mode, the city was painted through the wall of water. (7-36)

That cut, too, was pasted back into the final image. The silhouette of the city was used to make an opacity mask that was pasted into position. The original flat sky was removed and the stock sky was pasted in its place. (7-37)

Red lights were painted into the antenna to complete the image.

canvases were closed with the exception of the main canvas and the mask of the gold lines. Three additional identical canvases were created. In the color correction module, two of the three new canvases were altered. One was made approximately two f-stops darker and the other was made approximately two f-stops lighter than the normal canvas. The three new canvases were now the palette from which I was able to paint in the shadow and highlight areas on the final version. With the airbrush tool in the restore mode, I painted in the shadows around the eyelids, the muzzle, the mouth, and the forehead. The same technique was used for the highlights around the eyes and eyelids. For the final touch, the mask over the gold lines was turned on and reversed, leaving only the gold lines unmasked. Using the restore function once again with the lightest canvas, I added highlights to the metal strips, which made them pop and look convincingly metallic. (8-9)

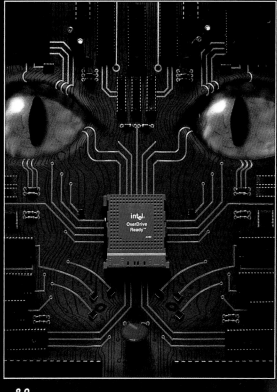

8-9

8-8

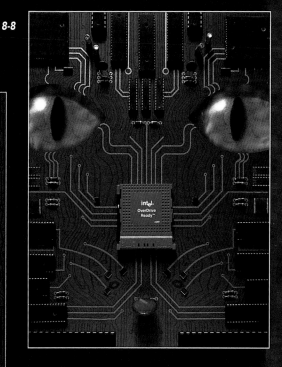

8-7

8-6

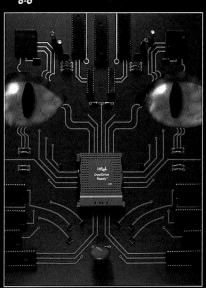

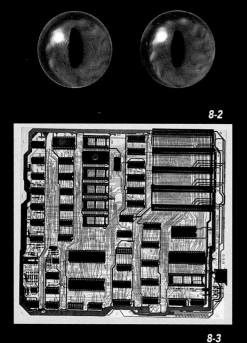

8-3

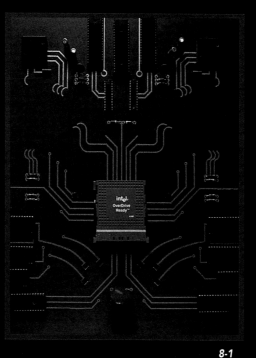

8-1

The chrome key function was used to isolate and generate the masking of a specific color. It was used to create masks that allowed me to separate the fine black lined circuitry from the rest of the real circuit board. This technique, however, produced large gaping holes that had to be filled by cloning from other parts of the image. Once the holes were filled, the most interesting area on the board was selected and mirror imaged until the canvas was filled. The green color of the model of the circuit board was matched and painted under the black lines. This gave me plenty to work with to create the contours of the cat's face. (8-7)

By isolating smaller areas of the canvass of fine black lines and cutting them out, I was able to use the warp function to create contour lines around the muzzle of the cat. The circuit board lines were used to follow the shape of the muzzle, the eye lids, and the rest of the face to create a dimensional effect reminiscent of the way a farmer plows a hill to prevent soil erosion. They were added to the main canvas after all the other objects on the board had been masked by using the chrome key masking function. (8-8)

Then the subtle final touches began. All the previous

8-4

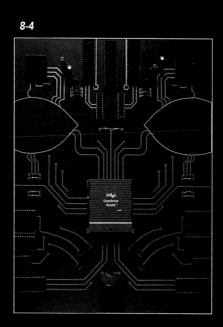

8-5

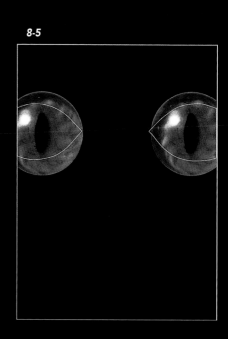

8

INTEL

CIRCUIT BOARD CAT FACE

How does one communicate longevity and durability after the alkaline rabbit has been preempted? One possibility was to go back to a more traditional symbol, a cat and its nine lives. The next challenge was how to integrate the cat with a circuit board in a clever and meaningful way. The art director's solution was to create the cat's head out of a circuit board and use parts of the board to represent parts of the cat's face. The result was a beautifully crafted and graphically simple image.

The circuit board that was the basis for the cat's face was created for the client by a model maker in California. Unfortunately, the masonite board, painted green, had none of the texture or translucent quality of a real circuit board. The lines that connected the chip's transistors were painted with gold paint. A red capacitor formed the tongue, and the product was the nose. (8-1)

We were able to get four pairs of glass cat eyes from a taxidermist in the city. The ones that were chosen had the best color. (8-2)

A photograph of real circuit board was selected as a source from which to transfer some realistic texture to the shot during the assembly process. (8-3)

The first step in the process was to create two identical canvases that matched the specified size of the final image and paste down the appropriately cropped circuit board model on them.

Whenever possible, I prefer to create a second or backup canvas for the one that I am working on rather than use the undo function. Most often it's one small part of what I have been working on that needs to be fixed or redone and the undo function tends to be an all or nothing kind of tool. Occasionally I use the backup canvas to bring back a ghosted image of the original area to blend with the current image.

An outline of what would be the open eyes were drawn in the line art mode to act as an overlay to guide the positioning of the eye components. (8-4)

A third canvas was created to host the eye components, and they were pasted down in position with the help of the overlay. Creating a separate canvas for the eyes would simplify the merging of the eyes with the board and would also facilitate the addition of shadows. The shadows were created by making a second set of eyes and making them the equivalent of several f-stops darker. Using the restore function, I was able to paint in the shadow of the upper lids from the darker version and still maintain color and detail in the shadow areas. (8-5)

Using the outline of the eyes in the line art module, masks of the two eye holes were created. The masks were then reversed to allow the painting of the eyes, with the shadows already in place, through the restore function. After the merging of the two canvases were completed, the eye canvases were closed. (8-6)

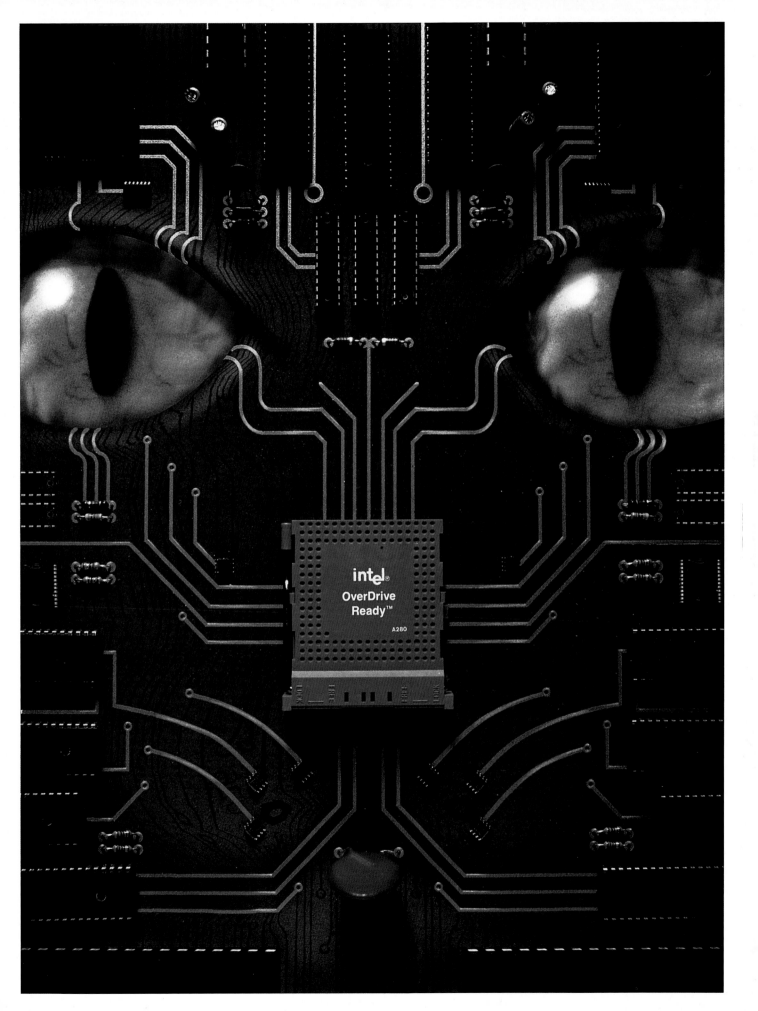

9

BARCO GRAPHICS

"METAMORPHOSIS" ADVERTISEMENT

Barco, a Belgian company, is well known internationally for its electronics. When it entered the graphic software market, it required establishing a new image for its new subsidiary company, Barco Graphics. As one of their first users in the United States, I was asked to come up with a concept for a visual that would incorporate as much of their system's capabilities in a single image as was possible. The evolution of the women's image, from the soft sexual object who would eventually become barefoot, pregnant, and whose place was in the kitchen, to the tough, independent, competitive career women of today who still has sensuality and motherhood as part of the mix, seemed like an appropriate allegory.

The evolution of a woman's image has not only been one of transformation but one of revelation. The naked torso, eternal symbol of soft sensuous femininity, peels away to reveal a brick torso symbolizing a new, tougher, competitive aspect to the female image to contemporary society. An hourglass is shown repeated in a continuous infinite trail as a continuum. Inside the hourglass is a more contemporary timepiece trickling into sand. The combination of the string of hourglasses and the contemporary clocks contained within represent the ages and the minutes in the continual passing of time. The point from which the torso rises is the center of a contemporary clock face about to strike the midnight hour, the traditional time of change. In the process of rising from the waters, eternal symbol of motherhood, the torso is partially shedding its sensuous shell as the metamorphosis progresses. The head consists of a transparent globe defined by a pattern of lips representing the stereotypical talkative female but reveals an inner sphere made of brick, strong, solid and mysterious.

In the tradition of Rene Magritte, the key components are ordinary familiar objects that, when assembled into a single image, become something much greater and more metaphorically meaningful than its components.

An alarm clock face representing contemporary time was chosen over a digital clock because, as an icon, it was much more visually interesting. Another reason was that it was a quicker read of a symbol for time than four numbers with a colon in the middle. It was also a much more dramatic image to have the minute hand about to strike the midnight hour than to have numbers reading 11:59. (9-1)

The shot of the woman's lips had to be full and sensual to give it the sexual symbolism that the image required. The model was selected accordingly. (9-2)

A photograph of white tufted clouds floating in a sea of blue was selected from my stock file of skies. It was a fortunate coincidence that the clouds trailed back forming a path to the horizon, which gave the hourglasses a line to follow. (9-3)

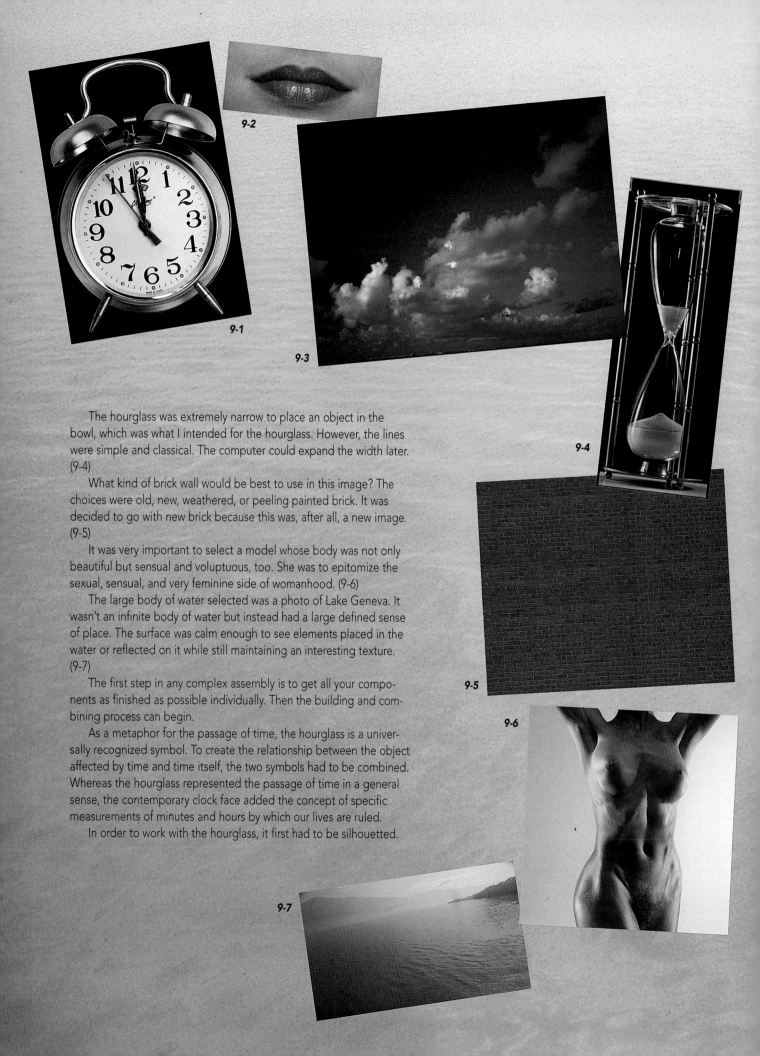

9-2

9-1

9-3

9-4

9-5

9-6

9-7

The hourglass was extremely narrow to place an object in the bowl, which was what I intended for the hourglass. However, the lines were simple and classical. The computer could expand the width later. (9-4)

What kind of brick wall would be best to use in this image? The choices were old, new, weathered, or peeling painted brick. It was decided to go with new brick because this was, after all, a new image. (9-5)

It was very important to select a model whose body was not only beautiful but sensual and voluptuous, too. She was to epitomize the sexual, sensual, and very feminine side of womanhood. (9-6)

The large body of water selected was a photo of Lake Geneva. It wasn't an infinite body of water but instead had a large defined sense of place. The surface was calm enough to see elements placed in the water or reflected on it while still maintaining an interesting texture. (9-7)

The first step in any complex assembly is to get all your components as finished as possible individually. Then the building and combining process can begin.

As a metaphor for the passage of time, the hourglass is a universally recognized symbol. To create the relationship between the object affected by time and time itself, the two symbols had to be combined. Whereas the hourglass represented the passage of time in a general sense, the contemporary clock face added the concept of specific measurements of minutes and hours by which our lives are ruled.

In order to work with the hourglass, it first had to be silhouetted.

Using the line art method for masking, the shape was outlined and filled with mask. The area surrounding the mask was removed. (9-8)

A new canvas was created, and the silhouetted hourglass was picked up in the paste-up mode and extended horizontally to create more space in which to place an object and still have it recognizable. To be able to see the pasted object through the glass and the inherent subtlety of the glass surface, the surface had to be made transparent. This was accomplished by painting the upper globe in the erase mode. By using a pressure sensitive stylus in the airbrush mode, it was possible to vary the amount of the transparency and control accurately, which areas were transparent, and how much transparency was applied. It was in this way that the sand was able to be removed and the reflections in the glass retained. The lower bulb was treated in the same way. Transparency was painted into the large plain areas of glass and less in the areas that contained reflections. The sand, of course, was left opaque. This would enable the background to be seen through the glass and created a convincing illusion of the hourglass existing in the environment in which it's placed. (9-9)

The clock face was separated from the alarm clock by laying a circular mask on its face and removing the surrounding area. It was then picked up with the warp tool and the bottom of the face was pulled downward to form a point. The lower half of the face was tapered to match the upper globe. (9-10)

With all the silhouetting and additional transparency completed, combining the two images was relatively easy. The tapered clock face was picked up in the paste up model and pasted in place under the hourglass after being downsized to fit the glass globe's shape. By pasting it under the image of the hourglass bulb, the characteristics of the glass and its reflections appeared over the clock face. This created the illusion that the clock face was contained inside. (9-11)

The term "3D" does not have the same meaning in the context of computer graphics as it does when used by the general population. To the general public, 3D is stereo-optical, wherein it creates the illusion of true depth from a two-dimensional surface, and objects seem to project out of the screen. In the context of computer graphics, 3D is a fully dimensional virtual object that is constructed and exists within the computer. This object has all the attributes of existence except touch. It can be rotated, lit, show reflections, create shadows and when covered with a skin of a photographic surface, look every bit as real as an object that is sitting on a table that can actually be picked up or touched. A wire frame of a globe was created in the 3D program. The photograph of the brick wall (9-12) was mapped to the globe's surface. To hide the seam, the point where the two opposing ends of the brick wall meet, the virtual brick globe was rotated until the seam was out of the field of view. (9-13)

The full, sensuous lips of the model had to be silhouetted. Chrome key auto masking was used to isolate the lips,

9-8

9-9

9-10

9-11

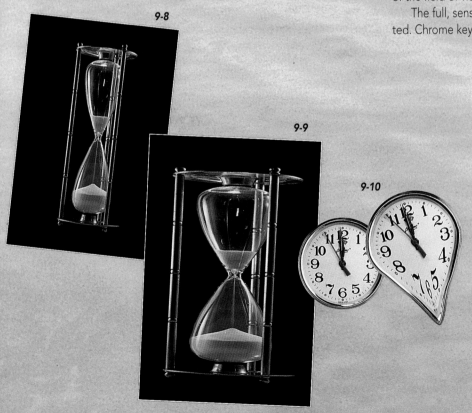

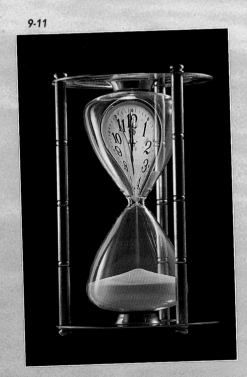

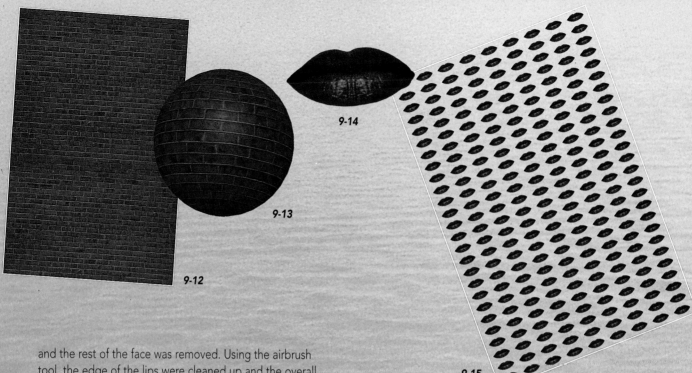

9-12

9-13

9-14

9-15

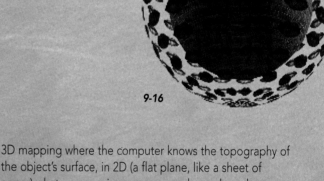

9-16

and the rest of the face was removed. Using the airbrush tool, the edge of the lips were cleaned up and the overall shape made perfect. The color was enriched in color correction by manipulating the curves. (9-14)

Using the capability of the computer to create patterns, a step and repeat pattern was made from the single image of the lips. The pattern floated on an empty canvas. The size to the pattern, the frequency of the repetition, and the size of the object repeated are all determined by the artist. The size of the pattern is determined by the canvas size, just as the size of the object repeated is determined by its size relative to the then new canvas on which the pattern will be created. Frequency of repetition is determined by the object size relative to the size of the original canvas on which the single object resides. (9-15)

A second larger wire frame sphere was created around the brick sphere. The skin of the second globe was made transparent. Onto the transparent skin, I mapped the pattern of lips creating brick globe surrounded by a sphere of floating lips. After the first globe was encased by the second, they had to be lit in a way to be consistent with the lighting on the model's torso. Within the 3D program are virtual lights that can be specified to duplicate spot, flood, or ambient lighting and be placed anywhere around the object. By placing two diffused floodlights on either side of the globe, I was able to reproduce the lighting on the globes that I used in the studio to photograph the model's torso. (9-16)

Turning a voluptuous torso into a brick sculpture was an incredible challenge. The mapping of a geometric pattern such as brick over a curvaceous surface required an accurate tracking of the contours, both vertically and horizontally. Another factor to consider was the perspective involved as the brick pattern edged around the side of the body to the back, or over and around the breasts. Unlike

3D mapping where the computer knows the topography of the object's surface, in 2D (a flat plane, like a sheet of paper) what we perceive as curves and roundness because of the indicators that represent in our minds, highlights and shadows are to the computer a flat pattern of light and dark. The computer has no way of interpreting those flat tonal areas as contours.

The first step, as it is with most components, was silhouetting the model's torso. To use the line art capability was the obvious choice because the outline was clean. After the mask had been applied, the background was removed. Then a duplicate canvas was created, and the torso was duplicated on it. (9-17)

All the contouring of the brick wall over the model's body had to be done by eye and hand with the warping tool. This was done because the computer could not recognize contours or dimensional shapes by reading the lights and darks of the object it was covering. (9-18)

Once the object was fully covered with the brick wall, and the horizontal and vertical pattern appeared to follow its contour, the highlights and shadows were brought over from the original torso. Using the computer's ability to bring areas of one image onto another through the restore function, I was able to carry over just the gray scale of the shadows to recreate the original contours of her body. (9-19)

Another duplicate canvas had to be made, this time of the brick torso. This enabled me to paint back areas that I didn't want covered with skin. Passing down the original skin image over the brick torso with the warping tool, I was able to pull down the skin as if it was being shed. It appeared to have a natural look as it stretched and distorted in a seemingly realistic way. (9-20)

The warping tool does not allow the image being warped to bend over itself. Folds and overlaps also have to be done by hand using paste-up or the cloning brush. The back part of the loose skin coming from behind her body was joined to the front part of the skin coming down from her right shoulder with paste-up and cloning techniques. (9-21)

The base of the torso where the legs enter the water had to be masked. I used line art to draw the water line as it flowed around the contours of the thighs, groin, and hips. The shape was closed and filled with masks, which was then inverted to erase the bottom part of the legs and body. It was necessary to remove the pubic hair because it was obvious that it would become a distracting focal point as a reflection on the surface of the water. The lines of the trunk where it met the legs also pulled the eye to it. (9-22)

The assembly began with the creation of a large canvas in proportion to the ad as it was going to appear in the magazine. Then the water was pasted into position. I wanted a vast expanse of water, but not quite an ocean. The lighting, the camera angle,

9-22

9-21

9-17

9-18

9-19

9-20

9-23

9-24

9-25

and even the texture of the water were perfect, however, the expanse of the water was not large enough. (9-23)

To check the color balance between the blue of the sky and blue of the water, the sky was also pasted into position. One color blue does not necessarily coordinate with another color blue. This was the case with the sky and the water. (9-24)

After creating a duplicate canvas, the surface volume of the water had to be increased. Taking advantage of perspective distortion to create the visual effect of multiplying the expanse of the water's surface many times over, I pasted the new water in position. This expansion of the surface made it possible to push the distracting bush in the lower right area of the picture out of the frame. I used the cloning brush to remove the bush from the bottom of the frame and turn the mountain ridge that trailed to the water's edge into a distant sliver. The mountain range in the background was not a problem since the sky was going to cover it. In the color correction module, the water's color was made deeper and brought into a range of blue that was complementary with the sky.

The first canvas of the old version of the sky and water was cleared, and the new expanded water was placed in position. Now that the colors worked together, the sky, too, was pasted in position. The distant mountains, which were a pale blue to begin with, were softened and were made ready to become part of the sky. Parts of the clouds were cloned and blended to expand the cloud base, making the merge with the distant mountains, now the sky, easier and eliminated any trace of the edge of the sky photo. (9-25)

The final image of the merged sky and water was duplicated on the backup canvas. An outline of the shape of the torso was made in line art

and was used as an overlay to experiment with its placement and its size relative to the total image. Once its size and position was determined, the hourglass component was fitted and pasted down. There was a minor amount of clean up in the lower bulb to create a clean and seamless joining of the two images that was accomplished with the cloning brush and by restoring the sky through the glass from the backup canvas. In some places the edges were too hard, which gave the image an artificial pasted up look. This undesired look was changed by painting the hard edges with a blurring brush. (9-26)

With the space that the torso would occupy clearly delineated, the hourglass components were pasted down. Each one was resized downward to create a feeling of perspective. As they became smaller, the color saturation was reduced to emphasize the great distance that the line covered. The hourglass components in the distance were also blurred slightly to create an out of focus rear plane. (9-27)

In preparation for the pasting of the torso in position, an opacity mask of the torso was created. This made it possible to paste down its mask at the same time as the torso and keep them both in perfect register. Once all the hourglass components were in place, the actual torso was pasted in position with its mask, and the line art guide was eliminated. (9-28)

An object's existence is evidenced, not only by its visual presence, but also by its affect on the objects surrounding it. Just as an object standing in a spotlight would cast a shadow over the plane on which it was standing and over any other secondary objects that were close enough to the main object to be covered by it, so would the torso affect the area surrounding it. This visual evidence not only confirms its existence but also gives it a sense of place. In the environment that the torso was placed, a shadow

9-29

would not have been as appropriate as a reflection on the surface of the water. By having made the torso and its reflection meet, the torso has been solidly and firmly placed in the water instead of appearing to float above it.

A second duplicate canvas was made with the torso and its mask in place. To create the illusion of a reflection on the surface of the water, the same original composite image of the torso was picked up in paste-up and inverted. It was pasted down with about 30 percent transparency that created a mirror image, allowing the color and texture of the water to be seen through it. (9-29)

The giant face of the contemporary timepiece, as the symbol of this modern era in which women emerge as the tough new competitive force shedding their previous image, was created from the same clock face component used in the floating hourglasses. To create the giant stage from which the torso emerged, first the clock face had to be rotated counterclockwise until it was in a position to align with the direction the torso was facing. The clock face was flattened with perspective distortion until the plane of the clock face matched the plane of the water. It, too, was pasted down with 30 percent transparency to allow the water's color, texture, and the torso's reflection to show through. (9-30)

The clock face and the torso reflection in the water were cut out and manipulated. Using the warping tool, the clock face and reflection were pulled, pushed, raised, and lowered to simulate the distortion caused by the uneven surface of the water. Some license regarding accuracy was taken to insure readability. The cut out was then pasted back into position. (9-31)

Finally, the last piece was added to the image. The concentric globes were sized and pasted into position to create the head. (9-32)

9-30

9-31

9-32

10

Rx

"RELEASING THE POWER OF THE PILL"

This is an example of an assignment that appears to be simple and straight forward. However, it is an impossible shot to make without a computer because of the technical realities and considerations involved. The concept is time release capsules replacing multi-dose pills. For the elderly who forget to take their pills every four hours, and for people who are too busy to stop to take their prescriptions at specific intervals, the time release capsules are a powerful aid to administering the proper dosage of medication. To symbolize this power, the size of the tiny spheres are exaggerated by altering the perspective.

The first problem in creating this image is the lack of depth of field when doing macrophotography. It would have been impossible to get the hands holding the capsule and the sphere closest to the lens in focus.

Secondly, it would have been just as impossible to get the tiny spheres of medicine to fall in a nice arrangement in the small area that could be captured on film.

The only part of this image that really exists, or to put it another way, a photograph of something that exists outside the computer, is the photographic component of the hands. After positioning the hand model, lighting the hands actually holding two halves of a real capsule, and taking Polaroids to check the lighting, the capsule halves were removed for the shoot. Since the spheres of medicine were going to be created in 3D, it made sense to create the capsule the same way. This would enable the capsule to have the same texture and color as the spheres it was supposed to contain. It also eliminated the problem of lighting small objects without ruining the overall lighting of the hands. (10-1)

Although the spheres and the capsule halves look photographic, they were created in the computer and lit as though they actually had substance and existed in the virtual photo studio created by computer software. (10-2)

The hands were cropped tightly to just show the fingers, as was called for in the layout. This shot, after all, is supposed to be macrophotographic in order to capture the tiny spheres that contain the medicine inside the capsule. They were also blurred slightly to give the impression of a slightly out of focus plane, enhancing the illusion of depth. (10-3)

The next step in the process was to create the two capsule halves the fingers are supposed to be holding. Two wire frame constructions were made of the shapes that were to be the capsule shells. They were rotated into position and viewed with different virtual wide angle lenses until the correct perspective and viewing angle was achieved and conformed with the fingers holding them. (10-4)

11

MSG

NEW YORK RANGERS POSTER

The Rangers were hot and getting hotter. Excitement was building in the city and in the surrounding areas. The function of the poster was to capitalize on this excitement and to attract new fans by capturing the speed and uniqueness of the game. Cliché phrases like "flying across the ice" and this team is "out of this world" became food for visual thought. Although the words were cliché, the visuals would not appear to be so.

Using their two big stars of the season, Brian Leach and the then newly acquired Bernie Nicholls, the idea was to have them skate through the sky like gods of hockey over the Manhattan skyline. The contrails from their skates implied speed, control, and from a design point of view, a nice line of movement indicating grace. The visual itself created a unique sense of excitement, as did the puck hurtling toward the camera.

We went with a sunlit day scene with a blue sky and white tufted clouds to create an atmosphere of hope and optimism, with which to the faithful fan, every season begins.

Delays in getting approval pushed our back up against the deadline wall. The images had to be shot, scanned, assembled, separated, printed, made into ads and posters, distributed to the media, and put up on the walls of the subways and bus stops with enough time to allow the public to buy the different season packages the Rangers were offering before the season began. The photography started with a hastily scheduled ride aboard the Staten Island Ferry. As long as it wasn't raining, I had to shoot the skyline. I knew that even a bright hazy day could be enhanced into a sunny day on my computer. Getting stock was an option, but I wanted a certain amount of "keystoning" of the buildings in the skyline. Keystoning is a one point perspective distortion of an object that is exaggerated by tilting a wide angle lens away from the object, placing it off center in the frame. It would have been extremely difficult to find just the right shot of the Manhattan skyline distorted in just the right way to work with the rest of the components in the image. It was actually more expedient to photograph it myself. (11-1)

When shooting several components for an assembly, always start with the component that can least be controlled in regard to lighting or angle of view. This approach makes it possible to maintain consistency throughout the assembled image. Once the skyline was photographed, the lighting and angle of view was established for the rest of the composition. The next components to be photographed were the Ranger players. Since they were airborne, skating in the sky, the angle of view had to be below ice or blade level. They had to be shot that way or the image would not ring true. A sheet of inch thick, 4 x 8 foot Plexiglas on supports held them five feet above me as I lay on the floor of my studio photographing them in full uniform and equipment. To get them into poses that were as natural as possible, I had them move and take shots

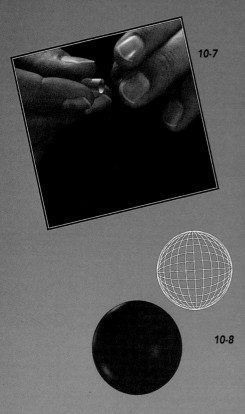

10-7

10-8

10-9

As the sphere is added to the image in the paste mode, the color of the surface is changed. To give the appearance of seeing the little spheres inside the capsule, the sphere is pasted down in different colors with a high degree of transparency. As they appear to cascade toward the viewer or camera lens, the relative sizes of the tiny spheres are made to grow larger, simulating perspective. (10-9)

The single sphere, changed in size and color but retaining the other characteristics that affect the entire image such as lighting and texture, was pasted down over and over again until the desired effect and volume is achieved. (10-10)

All the spheres and the fingers were pasted onto an empty canvas. Making a gradated background that traveled from dark to light blue and placing it behind the rest of the objects was achieved by creating the gradation in the under mode. (10-11)

10-10

10-11

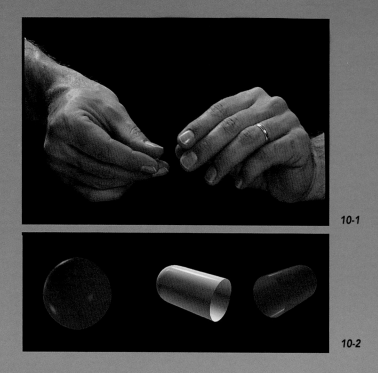

10-1

10-2

Once the qualities of the skins were selected from a choice of texture, color, and reflectivity, the skin was applied to the wire frames, A choice of lighting is also available in this virtual studio: ambient, flood, or spot. I chose a low ambient light with strong flood lighting to match the lighting of the hands. The selection of colors for the skin of the capsules were aesthetically driven. (10-5)

The capsule shells were sized to fit the scale of the hands and placed in position relative to the fingers that would be gripping them. (10-6)

In order to make the fingers look as though they are holding the capsule halves, the fingers must cover the cap-sule parts where they would be in place between the camera lens and the object they are holding. This was accomplished by creating a duplicate canvas of the fingers without the capsule halves. The parts of the object that should be covered by the fingers were painted over by transferring the fingers from the canvas that did not contain the capsule halves to the final canvas that did in order to create the desired effect. (10-7)

The spherical objects were created by making a wire frame ball. Texture, one color, and reflectivity of the object were selected. Having selected the parameters, the skin was wrapped or "mapped" onto the frame. (10-8)

10-3

10-4

10-5

10-6

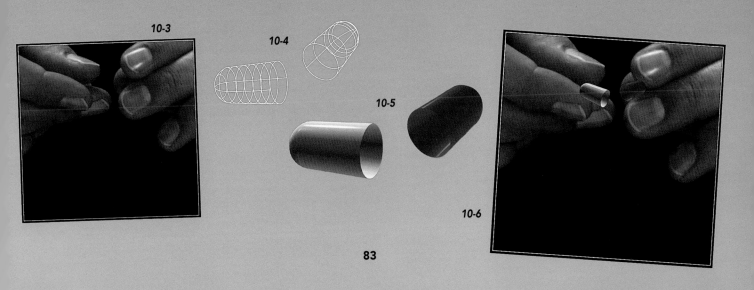

11-2

11-3

as if they were on the ice. This caused the Plexiglas to bend and bounce under their weight, the executives to worry about the welfare of their multimillion dollar stars plunging through a shattered sheet of Plexiglas, and me, who was under them, to fear for my life. The shoot went without a hitch. (11-2)

The puck was a tabletop shot, without movement. Movement would be added later, on computer, with much more control over the effect. (11-3)

A relatively clear blue sky with minimal tufted clouds was selected from my stock files. I wanted minimal clouds so as not to distract from everything else that was happening in the image. Lighting was also a factor in the selection process. (11-4)

Once all the selections were made, the transparencies were digitized and read into my computer where the first step, the silhouetting and color balancing of each component with the exception of the sky, was completed. (11-5)

The layout supplied by the agency was more conceptual than explicit. The Manhattan skyline was the foundation of the composition. Once the cropping, size, and placement of the buildings were decided, all the other components could be placed and sized. A canvas was created

11-5

11-1

11-4

11-6

that was proportional to the final size of the poster for which this image was being produced. The silhouetted cityscape was pasted into position. An outline tracing each Ranger was made. These were used to size and position the two figures in the sky, relative to each other and the city below. (11-6)

Each silhouetted figure was pasted into position. (11-7)

The puck was then sized and placed into position. It was inverted to allow the Rangers logo to be seen and was made much larger in scale for two reasons. The first was to feature the Ranger logo and the second was to give it a three dimensional coming-out-of-the-image-at-you effect. To create a sense of action and eye catching involvement between the poster and the viewer, more had to be done to the puck. However another step had to be done first. (11-8)

The sky had to be dropped behind the city, the puck, and the two figures. Since the assembled elements are pasted on an empty or transparent canvas, it was an easy process to add the sky in the under mode. It was necessary to add the sky before adding effects to the puck or Nicholls' stick because it's impossible to gauge subtlety of black object blurs against a black background. (11-9)

By cutting out the section of the image to be worked on, in this case the puck, a great deal of time was saved, and the working process was much less memory intensive. A duplicate canvas was created of the cutout portion of the total image. This

11-7

11-8

duplicate canvas was for backup, in case restoration of an area that didn't work was needed or to tone down an effect that may have been too heavy-handed. (11-10)

Using the cloning tool in the airbrush mode, I created the tracking trail by drawing the perspective using the outside edges of the puck. Starting with the top left to establish the line of movement, it was followed by the bottom left line and then the bottom right. (11-11)

Readjusting the direction of the cloning brush source, I filled in the remaining areas of the puck. The fade at the end of the trail was created by restoring, with medium transparency and a large airbrush, the original image from the duplicate canvas. (11-12)

The trail, however, was still relatively flat and needed to pick up some of the white in the center of the puck. This also allowed for an indication of spin, thereby giving the puck more motion and the total image more action. (11-13)

The cutout was then pasted back into position on the larger canvas. (11-14)

The same process was used to created motion in the stick held by Nicholls. First a cutout of the area to be worked on was made. (11-15)

A second, or duplicate, canvas of the cutout was made. (11-16)

The cloning brush tool was used to establish a general line and feeling of movement. (11-17)

As a final touch, the highlight was added with

11-14

11-13

11-12

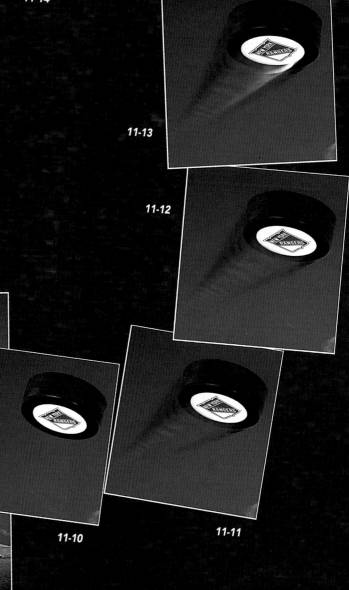

11-10

11-11

11-9

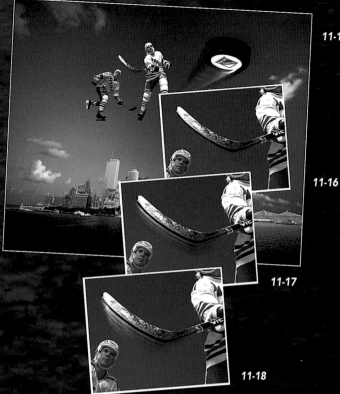

11-15

11-16

11-17

11-18

the cloning brush tool to create visual interest and break up the flat grayish look of the general motion trail. The fade at the end of the trail was achieved by restoring the image background from the duplicate canvas with a medium transparent airbrush. (11-18)

This altered cutout, too, was pasted down onto the original larger canvas. (11-19)

The final touches needed to tie the composition together were the contrails from the skates of the two Rangers. A duplicate canvas was created to control and correct the densities of the trails, but the undo function was also turned on while the lines that the three trails were to follow were drawn. Once the guidelines were drawn, accomplishing the goal of unifying the composition, the undo was turned off to conserve memory. The actual trails were drawn by hand using a very small diameter airbrush, starting with the skate blades and building in thickness as the contrail distanced itself from the skate. Photographs of real contrails emanating from jet plane engines were used as references. Although the contrails were painted in with some transparency, the effect of fading contrails behind the skyline and their transparency in front of the skyscrapers was mainly controlled and created by restoring from the duplicate canvas. (11-20)

11-19

11-20

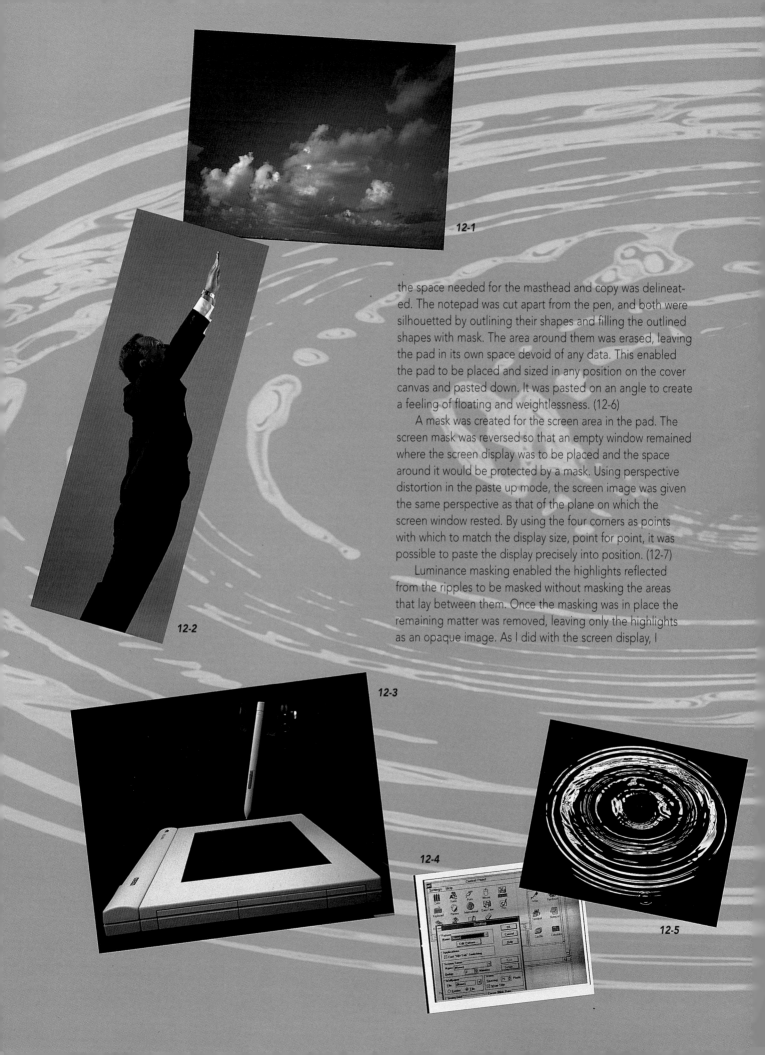

12-1

12-2

the space needed for the masthead and copy was delineated. The notepad was cut apart from the pen, and both were silhouetted by outlining their shapes and filling the outlined shapes with mask. The area around them was erased, leaving the pad in its own space devoid of any data. This enabled the pad to be placed and sized in any position on the cover canvas and pasted down. It was pasted on an angle to create a feeling of floating and weightlessness. (12-6)

A mask was created for the screen area in the pad. The screen mask was reversed so that an empty window remained where the screen display was to be placed and the space around it would be protected by a mask. Using perspective distortion in the paste up mode, the screen image was given the same perspective as that of the plane on which the screen window rested. By using the four corners as points with which to match the display size, point for point, it was possible to paste the display precisely into position. (12-7)

Luminance masking enabled the highlights reflected from the ripples to be masked without masking the areas that lay between them. Once the masking was in place the remaining matter was removed, leaving only the highlights as an opaque image. As I did with the screen display, I

12-3

12-4

12-5

12

VAR BUSINESS MAGAZINE

"DIVING INTO THE PEN MARKET" COVER

Suddenly, the marketplace exploded with LCD notepads that could store notes, doodles and diagrams. One could use the pen as a mouse for Windows programs and other applications, and some programs could read handwriting and convert it to printed text. They were new, and some, of course, worked better than others. Without question, these high-tech notepads were the latest status symbol for the cutting edge successful salesman or business executive.

Using the "liquid" from liquid crystal diode (LCD), which was how the screens displayed their data, as a starting point, the art director wanted to literally illustrate the cliché that best described the phenomenon that was taking place in the business world.

Since everyone was buying these notepads with the greatest of expectations, the only logical sky to have as the background was a rich blue one with large white tufted clouds. Of course, it had to leave enough space for the masthead, the name of the magazine, the headline, and the cover copy. This one was selected from my stock file of blue skies. (12-1)

I had two choices in shooting the diving executive. The first was to hang the model by his ankles from the ceiling of the studio and use a fan and thin nylon fishing line to fight gravity and give the feeling of wind and momentum, forcing his loose clothing in the opposite direction of his line of forward motion. The second option was to let gravity do all the work and have the model stand upright in a diving position aiming at the ceiling. As tempting as the first option was, I went with the second. (12-2)

The digital pen and notepad were shot as a single image instead of two separate shots. It made the lighting consistent, the perspective believable, and the proportions of the pen and pad accurate. Here, however, I had to fight gravity with clamps and tape. (12-3)

It was necessary to show a typical display of a Windows application that would be the largest usage of digital notepads and pens. The display was shot directly on the screen from a straight on viewing angle. An unexpected plus was the way the screen photographed. It turned blue and purple, which helped the illusion of the screen being a pool of liquid when combined with liquid ripples. (12-4)

The ripples were shot by filling a basin, painted black, with water. A single strobe head was positioned over it so that the ripples would catch the light but the surface would not act as a mirror to reveal the head itself. Finding the correct angle and position was done by trial and error, and Polaroids. The next step was the timing of the exposure. The trick was to wait for the moment when the ripples were at their widest and just before the counter ripples started to come back from the walls of the basin. (12-5)

After creating a canvas proportional to the cover with a little extra area to allow for bleed,

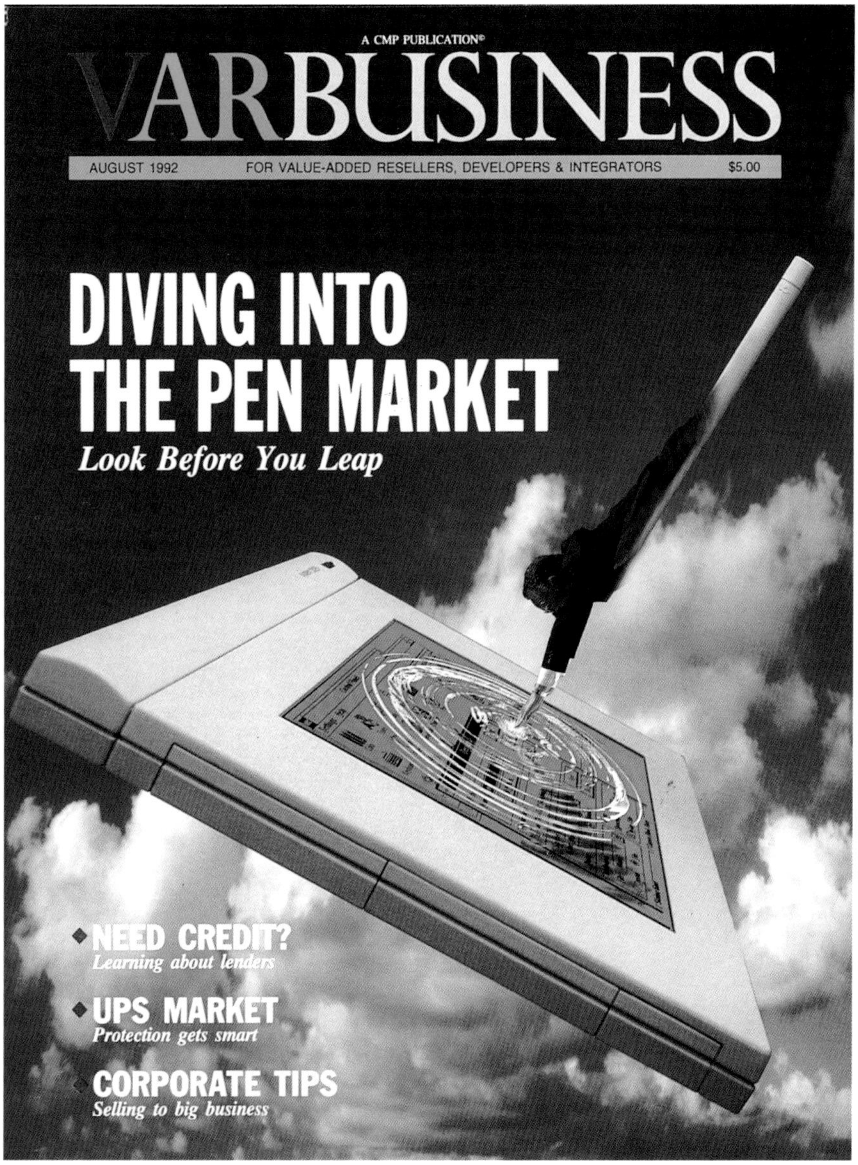

A CMP PUBLICATION®

VARBUSINESS

AUGUST 1992   FOR VALUE-ADDED RESELLERS, DEVELOPERS & INTEGRATORS $5.00

DIVING INTO THE PEN MARKET

Look Before You Leap

◆ **NEED CREDIT?**
Learning about lenders

◆ **UPS MARKET**
Protection gets smart

◆ **CORPORATE TIPS**
Selling to big business

applied perspective distortion to the ripple canvas to match the screen plane and placed the image over the screen window. The image was pasted down once all the corner points were matched. With the transparent space between the highlights, the display was visible and the screen appeared to be made of liquid. (12-8)

When the pen was cut out to separate it from the pad, a new canvas that contained the pen was created. The pen was masked and silhouetted by removing everything surrounding it to create an empty background field. (12-9)

The image of the male model was silhouetted by outlining him and filling in the shape with mask. In the same way that the pen was isolated in a field of emptiness, so too, was the background surrounding the male model erased. A duplicate canvas was made of the pen canvas. The image of the male model was inverted, sized to the pen, and pasted onto the duplicate canvas in a position that corresponded to

12-8

12-7

12-6

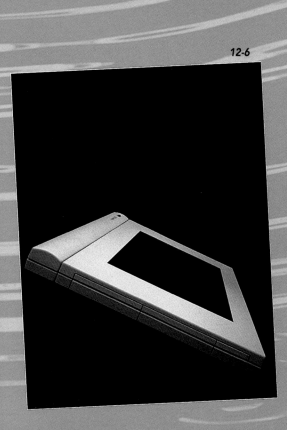

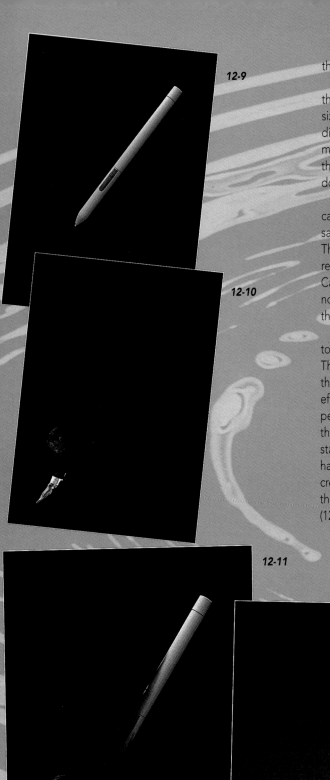

12-9

12-10

12-11

12-12

12-13

the place it would occupy when combined with the pen. (12-10)

A third canvas was created, identical in size to the ones of the pen. On this canvas, the pen was pasted in the position and size that was identical to the first. Using the airbrush tool, the diving man was painted over the pen in the restore mode. The man's head, arms, and shoulders were painted as opaque over the pen. His body became more transparent as it was painted down the barrel until it disappeared into the pen. (12-11)

The pen/man was pasted into position on the final cover canvas. Care was taken to be sure the pen was resized at the same percentage as the pad, creating accurate size proportion. The sky was pasted down behind the pen and pad. This was the reason for making the background transparent for both objects. Careful positioning of the cloud image to assure there would be no conflict with the cover copy yet it interacted aesthetically with the main subjects was a primary concern. (12-12)

Two subtle but very important items remained to be added to the image in order to create a sense of reality and substance. The first, to create the sense of reality, was to put a reflection of the pen/man on the surface of the screen. To maintain the ripple effect, the highlight mask was pasted into position. Then the pen/man cutout was inverted and pasted into the position where the reflection would appear. Second, to give the pen/man substance and the ripples a rational reason for being, the fingers had to make contact with the surface. This was evidenced by creating a splash. The splash was created by painting it in with the airbrush tool and using a paint sample from the ripple. (12-13)

13

TIME WARNER CABLE

"IT TAKES A LOT TO SURPRISE A NEW YORKER"

Playing on the reputation that New Yorkers have for being unflappable, the concept of this campaign was that the service from Time Warner Cable was so good that even cynical and hardened New Yorkers would be surprised. To illustrate the point a New York City landmark, the lions in front of the New York Public Library, were selected to come alive atop their pedestals without the passing natives taking notice.

Two shoots were necessary to create this image. It is always a good idea to shoot the part of the composition wherein the photographer has the least control over a factor that affects the entire image and all the elements have to be keyed to it. Sometimes it is the angle of view that is limited and all the components have to conform to the perspective that the photographer is forced to use. At other times, as in this case, it is the available light that has to be consistent.

The library was shot first. In scouting the area, I found that at the time of year we were shooting, the sun would only be in the right position for about 45 minutes beginning 11:45 A.M. That meant we had to shoot through the lunch hour when the steps and the streets would be the most crowded. Since this was an ad, we couldn't have any recognizable people in it without a model release. We had a permit from the city to shoot but not obstruct the movement of the public on the property of the library. The security guards of the library made sure that we didn't. It also meant that we had to shoot quickly with only 45 minutes of light before the surrounding skyscrapers would cast shadows across the set. In that time we had two different setups to shoot that had to work together when the image was assembled. The models that were hired had to change outfits and the women also had to change their hairstyles between setups to appear as different people in each shot.

The first shot was the lion in the foreground, shot low with a moderate wide angle lens to give it a heroic perspective for drama and interest. We only had time for two variations in this setup, and we ended up combining the two in the final assembly. This lens also pushed the second lion so far back it was almost out of the scene, which was the reason for the second setup. (13-1) (13-2) Although we moved the camera half way across the steps, the angle of the camera and the perspective of the steps had to be identical to the first setup so that our cheating would be undetectable. (13-3)

The lion model was also the model for the animated movie, *The Lion King*, and was brought up from Florida for the shoot. We rented a large studio to accommodate the cage as well as the platform we built to match the height of the library's pedestals. It was small comfort, kneeling before a full grown lion, to hear the trainer tell me not to move if the lion should pounce—that they would move quickly before he ate too much. We shot the lion with variations of what we

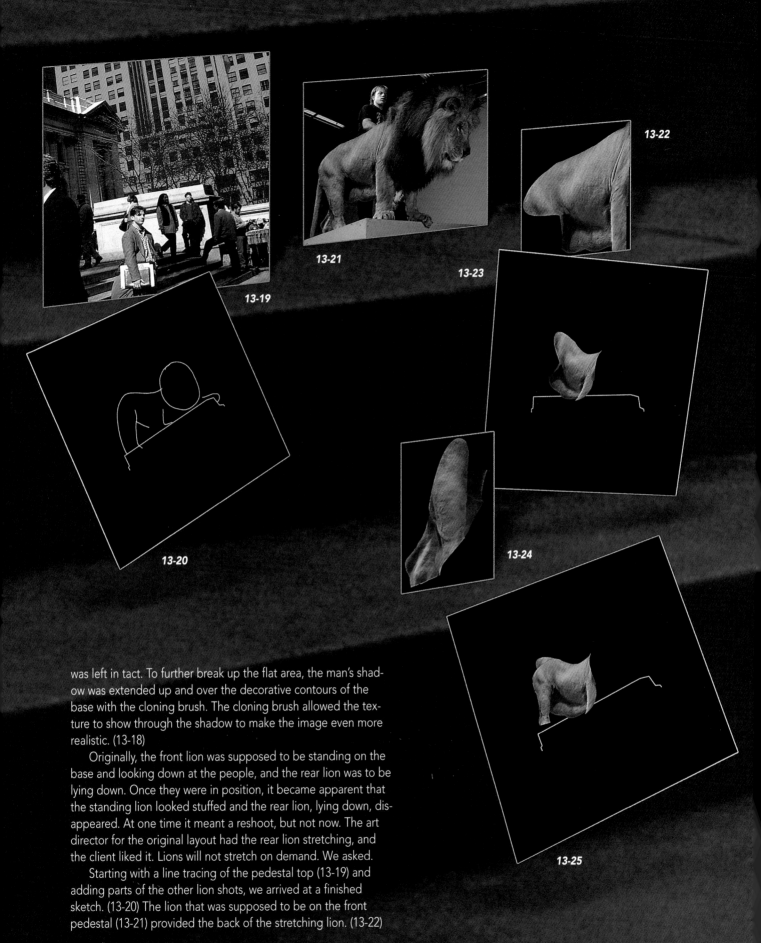

13-19

13-21

13-22

13-23

13-20

13-24

13-25

was left in tact. To further break up the flat area, the man's shadow was extended up and over the decorative contours of the base with the cloning brush. The cloning brush allowed the texture to show through the shadow to make the image even more realistic. (13-18)

Originally, the front lion was supposed to be standing on the base and looking down at the people, and the rear lion was to be lying down. Once they were in position, it became apparent that the standing lion looked stuffed and the rear lion, lying down, disappeared. At one time it meant a reshoot, but not now. The art director for the original layout had the rear lion stretching, and the client liked it. Lions will not stretch on demand. We asked.

Starting with a line tracing of the pedestal top (13-19) and adding parts of the other lion shots, we arrived at a finished sketch. (13-20) The lion that was supposed to be on the front pedestal (13-21) provided the back of the stretching lion. (13-22)

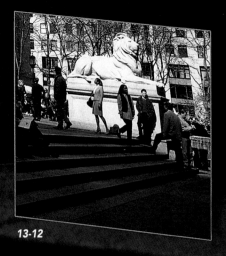

13-12

13-15

13-16

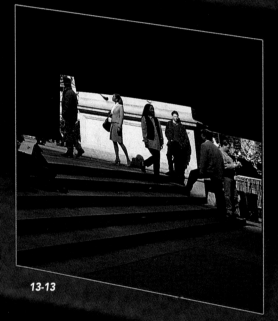

13-13

13-17

13-18

13-14

books and the sunny steps replaced the rear shot steps that were in shadow. Where background was needed to fill the void left by the missing lion, the background was cloned. (13-14)

To fill in the glaring white panel on the foreground pedestal, I replaced the couple sitting on the bench with the same couple from the alternate setup in which the man with the cellular phone is standing. A cutout of the couple plus the area to contain a shadow was made from the alternate shot. (13-15) The man next to the model with the phone was painted out of the picture by cloning from the pedestal facade around him. (13-16) Using the restore capability, the couple was painted over the original seated couple, (13-17) but the original background

13-7

13-8

13-9

13-10

ter shot was created for the restore capability, which was used when the different elements were combined. (13-11)

A cutout of the area to be worked on was made. The rear lion was easier to remove because less background had to be created owing to the different angle of view that the foreground shot provided. It was into the foreground or master shot that this image would be placed. (13-12) Everything that wasn't needed for the combined images of foreground and background was erased, thereby leaving the background empty, to be filled by the master shot. (13-13) The steps were lined up with the master shot for registration and pasted down. Using the restore capability, the man in the foreground was painted over the person sitting on the steps. The student with his

13-11

13-4

13-5

13-6

13-1

13-3

13-2

thought would be the foreground pose (13-4)(13-5) and the rear pedestal pose. We were wrong. (13-6)

Removing the lion from the pedestal was easy. I cut out the area to be worked on to save time and valuable memory. (13-7) I created an outline mask, reversed it, and erased the lion. (13-8) The hard part was filling in the hole that the lion left by recreating the part of the building that the lion had blocked. That was done by cloning the parts of the building that were visible and filling in the void. (13-9) Shadows cast by the sculptured paws were left to paint in different shadows with the cloning brush once the live lion was in place. (13-10) The empty pedestal was put back into the master shot to await the lion. A duplicate canvas of the mas-

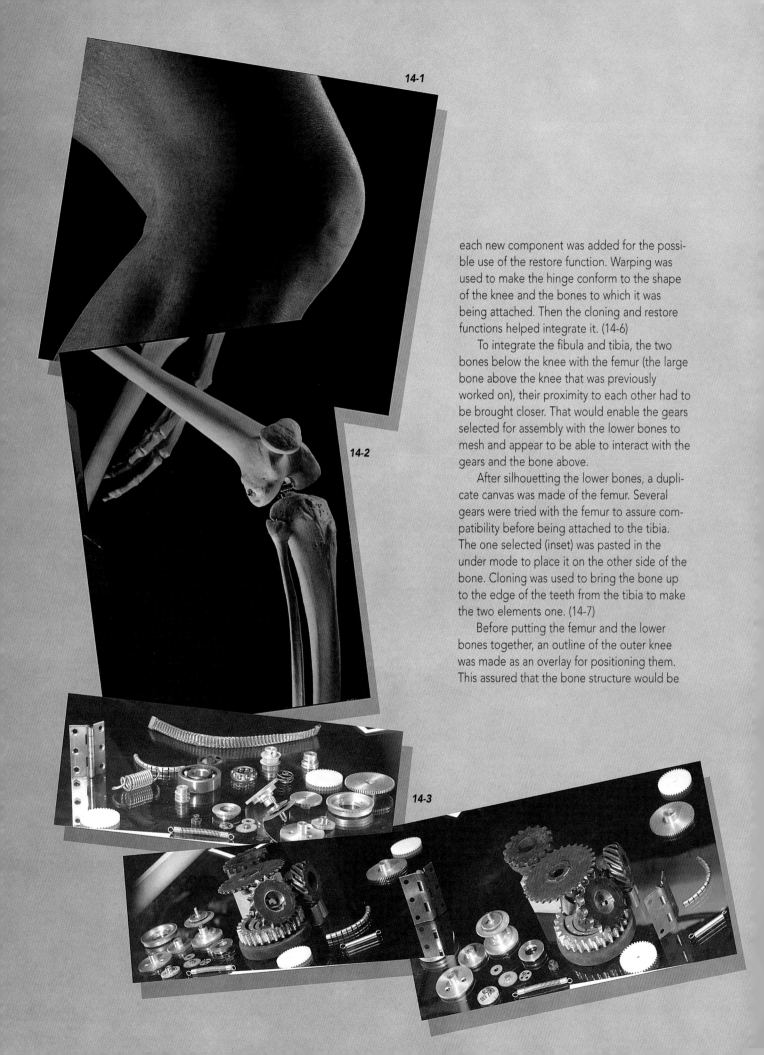

14-1

14-2

14-3

each new component was added for the possible use of the restore function. Warping was used to make the hinge conform to the shape of the knee and the bones to which it was being attached. Then the cloning and restore functions helped integrate it. (14-6)

To integrate the fibula and tibia, the two bones below the knee with the femur (the large bone above the knee that was previously worked on), their proximity to each other had to be brought closer. That would enable the gears selected for assembly with the lower bones to mesh and appear to be able to interact with the gears and the bone above.

After silhouetting the lower bones, a duplicate canvas was made of the femur. Several gears were tried with the femur to assure compatibility before being attached to the tibia. The one selected (inset) was pasted in the under mode to place it on the other side of the bone. Cloning was used to bring the bone up to the edge of the teeth from the tibia to make the two elements one. (14-7)

Before putting the femur and the lower bones together, an outline of the outer knee was made as an overlay for positioning them. This assured that the bone structure would be

14

TYLENOL

"FOR THE MECHANICAL PAIN OF OSTEOARTHRITIS"

Symptoms of arthritis include joint inflammation and pain. It has been described as a rusty misaligned hinge or an old gear box with some of the gears missing teeth. That was the concept the client wanted to illustrate, but they were not sure what form the hinge or gear box should take. At one time this would have been a job for a model maker. The problem with a model is that if there isn't a clear idea what the model should look like, changes become prohibitively expensive down the line. Computer imagery makes the process much more fluid.

The only definite image decision was that a knee and its shape were to be featured in the ad. What the interior of the knee was supposed to look like was still undecided. How much metal and how much bone were still points of conjecture. After much discussion, we decided to build the interior of the knee on the computer as we went along. I would do the basic construction and then we, the art director, and occasionally the account people and the client, would consult as the building process continued.

A knee of a 70-year-old female model was shot to fit the layout. (14-1)

The leg and knee joint of a rented skeleton were photographed in a similar pose to the photo of the human knee. (14-2)

For the remaining bits and pieces, my assistant went shopping from store to store buying used gears, springs, hinges, and metal straps. We went through them and picked a cross section, from old to new. Since we had no idea how they were going to be used, we photographed them at different angles with general lighting. (14-3)

A cutout was made of just the knee area that would be worked on, and a second duplicate canvas was created to use for the restore function, which I prefer over the undo capability. (14-4)

Various gears were cut out of the group shots. Each one was tried in the paste mode set to semi-transparent so that it was possible to see exact placement and relationship between the bone and gear. Experimentation involved trying different sizes and angles until one worked (inset). The gear was silhouetted and pasted into position. To make the gear part of the bone and the structure of the knee, judicious use of the cloning and restore functions were applied to the image. In every case, paint applied with a texture brush was used to give the metallic components a worn and rusted look. (14-5)

The hinge came next (inset). It was easier to work from the front to back for visualization purposes, but technically more difficult because it meant working around the shape that preceded the one that was being added to the composition. The duplicate canvas was updated before

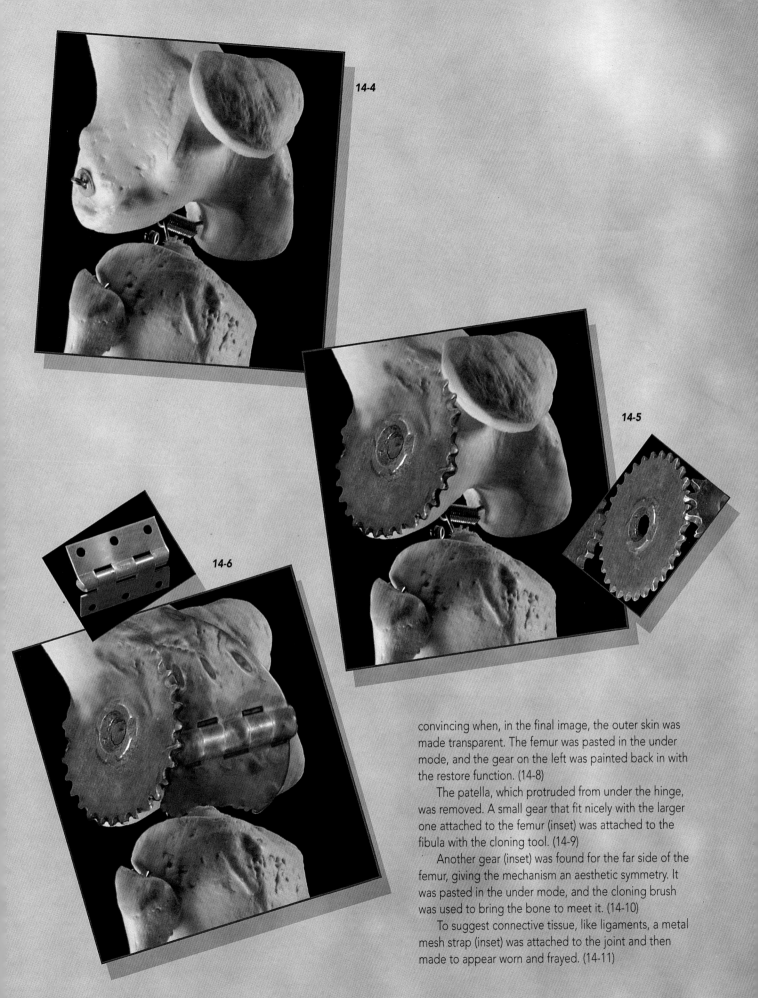

14-4

14-5

14-6

convincing when, in the final image, the outer skin was made transparent. The femur was pasted in the under mode, and the gear on the left was painted back in with the restore function. (14-8)

The patella, which protruded from under the hinge, was removed. A small gear that fit nicely with the larger one attached to the femur (inset) was attached to the fibula with the cloning tool. (14-9)

Another gear (inset) was found for the far side of the femur, giving the mechanism an aesthetic symmetry. It was pasted in the under mode, and the cloning brush was used to bring the bone to meet it. (14-10)

To suggest connective tissue, like ligaments, a metal mesh strap (inset) was attached to the joint and then made to appear worn and frayed. (14-11)

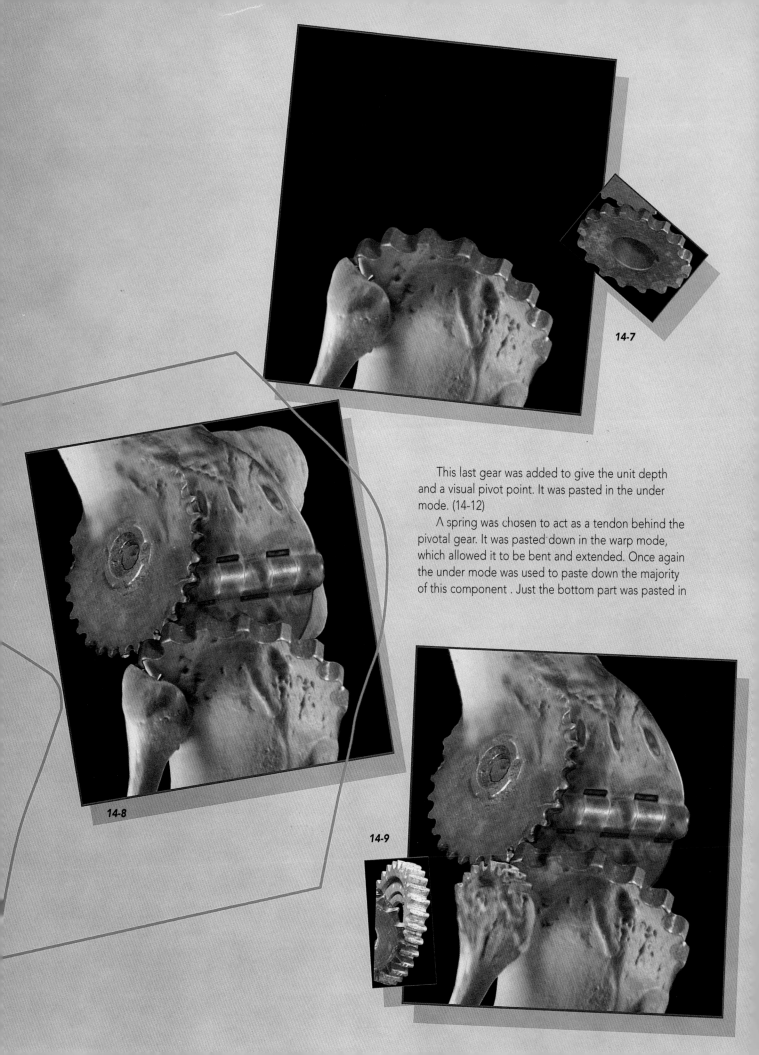

14-7

This last gear was added to give the unit depth and a visual pivot point. It was pasted in the under mode. (14-12)

A spring was chosen to act as a tendon behind the pivotal gear. It was pasted down in the warp mode, which allowed it to be bent and extended. Once again the under mode was used to paste down the majority of this component . Just the bottom part was pasted in

14-8

14-9

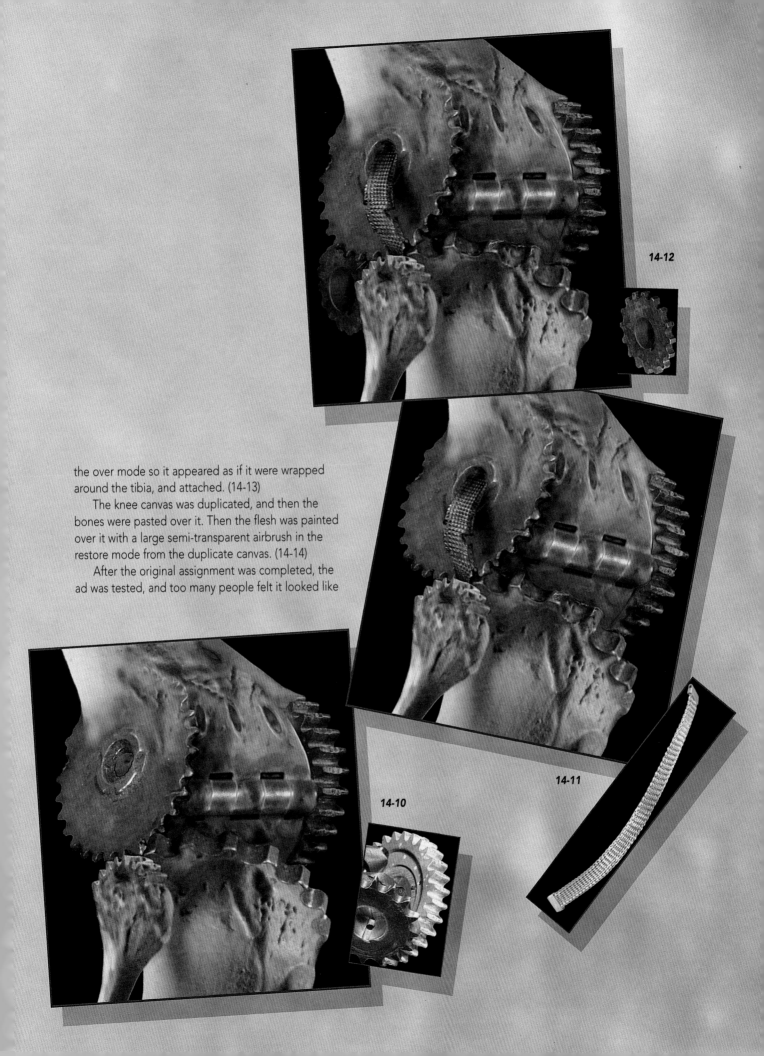

14-12

the over mode so it appeared as if it were wrapped around the tibia, and attached. (14-13)

The knee canvas was duplicated, and then the bones were pasted over it. Then the flesh was painted over it with a large semi-transparent airbrush in the restore mode from the duplicate canvas. (14-14)

After the original assignment was completed, the ad was tested, and too many people felt it looked like

14-11

14-10

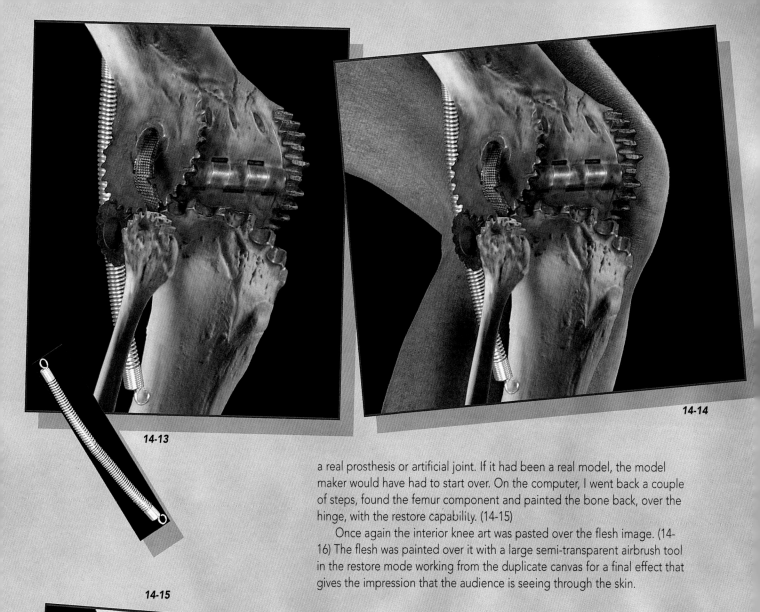

14-13

14-14

a real prosthesis or artificial joint. If it had been a real model, the model maker would have had to start over. On the computer, I went back a couple of steps, found the femur component and painted the bone back, over the hinge, with the restore capability. (14-15)

Once again the interior knee art was pasted over the flesh image. (14-16) The flesh was painted over it with a large semi-transparent airbrush tool in the restore mode working from the duplicate canvas for a final effect that gives the impression that the audience is seeing through the skin.

14-15

14-16

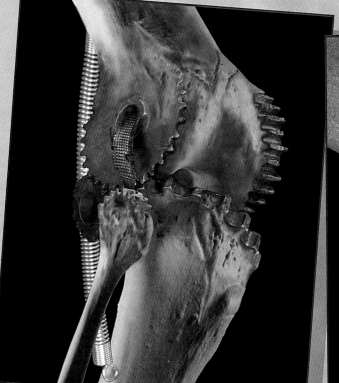

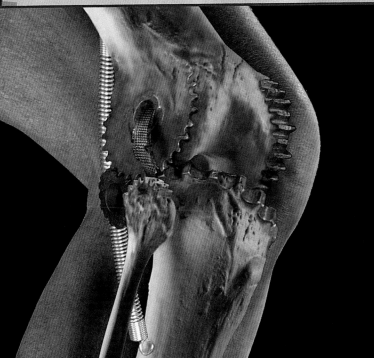

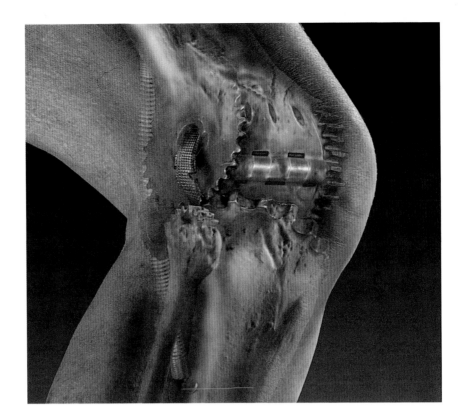

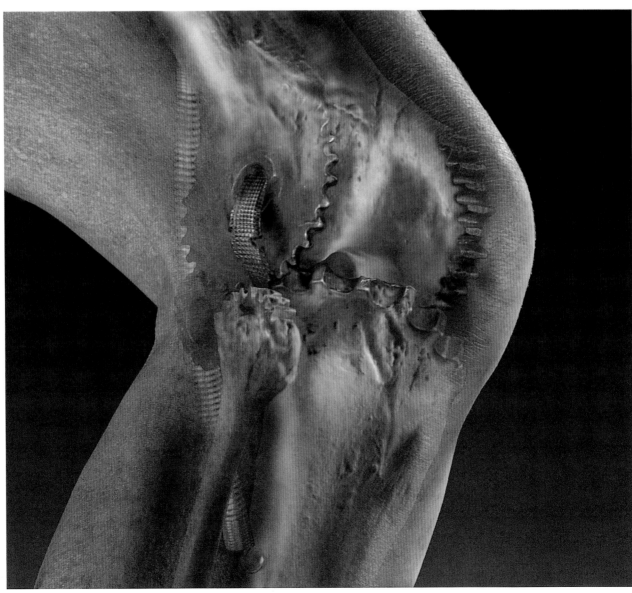

15

VASELINE INTENSIVE CARE

SKIN RELIEF

The words dry, chapped, rough, cracked, burning, and red are used to describe the symptoms of skin in an unfortunate state. Cooling, soothing, soft, smooth, silky, creamy, refreshing, moist, and healing are words that are used to describe how Intensive Care lotion feels on the skin that is in that unfortunate state. The visual communication of that very message in a unique eye-catching way was the assignment. Digital photographic illustration was the way to do it. Using symbols to create a sensorial empathy with the message, instead of the usual verbal intellectual communication of the message, is communication on a most profound level.

The photography for this image was straightforward. A table top set up of the product was all that was called for. Soft directional lighting was added to give the product volume and interest. Color manipulation is almost always done on computer as a later step in the process. To put gels or filters on the lights or camera lens narrows the options available should a better idea or a change of heart come along once the shoot has ended. (15-1)

Lighting for the hands, however, had to be more specific to achieve a convincing end result. The palms of the hands were illuminated by a direct, bright light source. A more general, almost ambient light illuminated the back of the hands and arms. No color alteration was used at this point for the same reasons previously stated. (15-2)

Having a large stock resource of skies, textures, and subjects saves a tremendous amount of time and money for me and my clients in terms of usage fees, accessability, and availability of images. The sunset was chosen to represent a hot dry atmosphere. (15-3)

Blue skies and white clouds, on the other hand, represent a cool, ideal, pleasant condition. (15-4)

A photograph of a parched, cracked, and lifeless piece of earth does not need to have its symbolism explained in the context of a moisturizer. The contrast is obvious and helps to visually hammer home the point of how bad dry skin feels. (15-5)

This shot of the surface of a pool with its cool, crystal clear blue water, is the perfect counter point to the dry cracked earth. (15-6)

A canvas of the proportional size as the final illustration would appear in print was created. From the tracings of the different components, a master sketch was made that came close to the layout. The sketch was sized to the canvas and saved as an overlay to make the composite. (15-7)

The photograph of the cracked desert earth was flattened in the perspective correction paste mode to create the plane on which the product would be able to stand. One point perspective was used that diminished the size of the detail in the distance and created the illusion that the land was actually photographed from that point of view. (15-8)

15-1

15-2

15-3

15-4

15-5

With the creation of this plane, a site for placement of the product was also created. The product was silhouetted, sized to the layout, and then pasted into it. (15-9)

A duplicate canvas was created. The layout was turned on and the primary canvas was picked up in the warp paste mode. The product was then bent to conform to the layout and pasted down on the new canvas. (15-10)

Another duplicate canvas was created. After the hands were silhouetted, they were sized to the layout and the product. The hands were then pasted onto the third canvas in the position to be used for merging the hands with the product on the primary canvas through the restore paint mode. (15-11)

Before starting the merge of the hands with the product, a duplicate canvas of the warped product was created in case the product had to be repainted over the hands. Using the airbrush to transfer the image of the hands, the combination of the two was done gradually to achieve a smooth transition from product to hand. (15-12)

It was necessary to jump back and forth between the product canvas and the hands canvas several

15-6

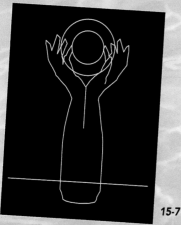

15-7

15-8

times, using the restore mode to get the proper transition on the primary canvas. (15-13)

Using a 3D program, a wire frame of a small globe was created. The photograph of the water surface was mapped to, or wrapped around, the wire frame to produce a water-covered globe. A silhouette version of the cloud image was created by masking the blue sky. I inverted the mask to leave the blue exposed and the clouds masked, which made it easy to erase the sky background. Another larger globe wire frame was produced around the smaller water globe. The clouds, which were now floating in a transparent field, were mapped onto the larger globe producing a water globe surrounded by a sphere of clouds. (15-14)

The overlay was brought back for the placement of the globe in the hands, and the globes were pasted into position. With the secondary canvas of the hands in place, the thumbs were painted over the clouds utilizing the restore function, thereby, placing the globes in the middle of the hands. (15-15)

Once the globe was pasted into position, all the secondary canvases were deleted. A new backup duplicate canvas was created of the assembly with the globes in it. (15-16)

A color shift was added to the primary canvas turning it very warm. Two small cutouts were made of the hands and the globes. One was color shifted to the cool side, the other to the warm side.

15-9

15-10

15-11

15-12

15-13

15-14

15-15

15-16

15-17

15-18

15-19

Utilizing the restore function in the paste mode, the cool white color was transferred by airbrush from the small cutouts to the palms of the hands. The soft edge of the airbrush diminished the chance of a hard edge between the warm and cool tones of the hands.

A cutout of the base was made and darkened with the use of the color correction module. The restore function allowed the darker cracked earth in the cut to be painted over the normal cracked earth on the primary canvas, producing a shadow. (15-17)

The sunset had to be made even hotter to exaggerate the heat surrounding the coolness of the globes and the surface of the inner hands. This was done by manipulating the color correction curves and pumping up the red. (15-18)

In the paste mode, the sunset width was compressed to exaggerate the height and pasted down in the under mode to put it behind the hands, globes, and the land. The final step was to increase the contrast just slightly to make it snap. (15-19)

16

TELEGRAPH COLOR LIBRARY

"I CHANGED MY MIND"

This image, created for my stock agency, is not the extreme or highly stylized imagery that is usually associated with digital photographic illustration. If it wasn't for the danger involved in setting up a shoot like this, there is no reason to believe that this was an altered photograph. The image in its final form exhibits no evidence of being manipulated. The point is that it wasn't necessary to risk life and limb to get the photographic image. What the mind can conceive the camera, the computer, and the artist can achieve quickly, economically, effectively, and safely.

The model was originally shot as if he were falling. He was supported only across his shoulders and at the small of his back. This support structure allowed his clothes to fall freely and his limbs to extend naturally. The camera was mounted 14 feet high on a scaffold. (16-1)

The street scene was shot hanging out of a window in mid-Manhattan. The most difficult challenge was finding a corner office 30 floors up with a window that opens. Having the photo of the model made it easy to match the camera angle. This was an important consideration in having the perspective of the surrounding buildings match the angle of view relative to the model. (16-2)

When I did a rough assembly, the image was so realistic and the model looked so terrified, I found the resulting picture too disturbing for stock. He needed an element of hope, a chance of rescue. Instead of calling the model back for a reshoot, I shot my assistant's hand gripping a board from an angle similar to where his hand would be relative to his body if he had caught hold of a ledge. (16-3)

What ledge? There was no ledge. To make my life less problematic, I photographed a concrete slab in a park near my studio. It was messy, with debris that could find its way to a ledge that obviously would not be swept and which had a collection of bird droppings. (16-4)

While I was there a pigeon showed up. One should always be open to unexpected inspirations. Having a pigeon watching the model's predicament could lighten up the ominous situation. I snapped a few shots of the bird from the top of a park bench before it took off, just in case it would work. (16-5)

The assembly started with the shot of the streets below. There was some flexibility as to how the model could be positioned, and nothing could be put together until the ledge was created. (16-6)

Turning a slab of concrete into a ledge required that the slab be cut into a long rectangle (inset). The edges had to look worn and weathered. This effect was achieved by darkening the edges with the airbrush tool using a dark color picked up from one of the dark spots on the slab, and by rounding off the corners. Strictly for aesthetics and visual interest, two slabs were used, instead of one, and were placed slightly out of alignment. (16-7)

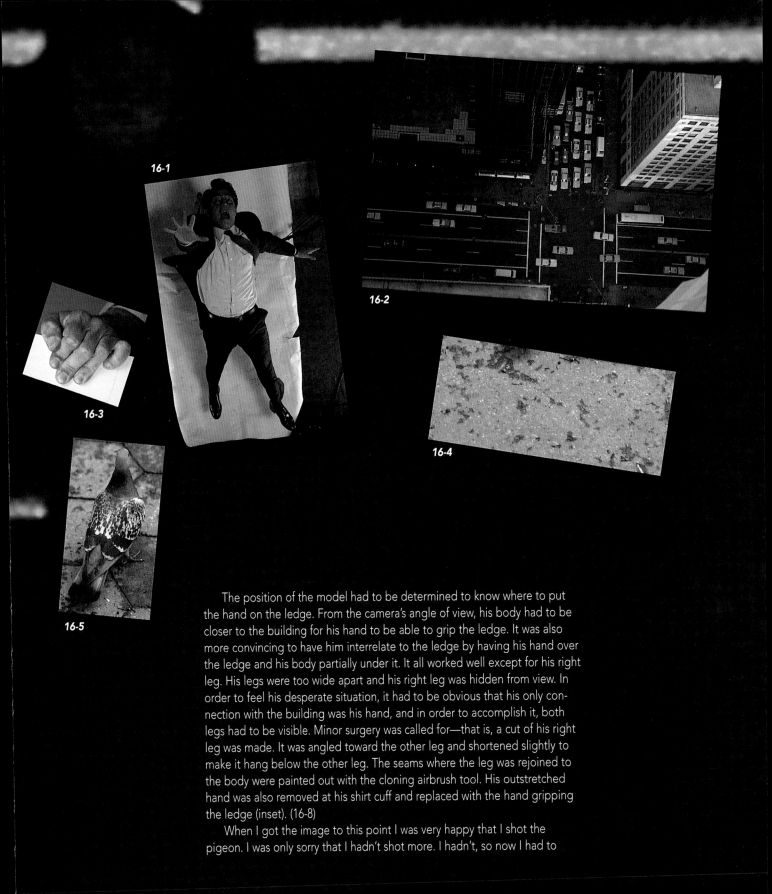

16-1

16-2

16-3

16-4

16-5

The position of the model had to be determined to know where to put the hand on the ledge. From the camera's angle of view, his body had to be closer to the building for his hand to be able to grip the ledge. It was also more convincing to have him interrelate to the ledge by having his hand over the ledge and his body partially under it. It all worked well except for his right leg. His legs were too wide apart and his right leg was hidden from view. In order to feel his desperate situation, it had to be obvious that his only connection with the building was his hand, and in order to accomplish it, both legs had to be visible. Minor surgery was called for—that is, a cut of his right leg was made. It was angled toward the other leg and shortened slightly to make it hang below the other leg. The seams where the leg was rejoined to the body were painted out with the cloning airbrush tool. His outstretched hand was also removed at his shirt cuff and replaced with the hand gripping the ledge (inset). (16-8)

When I got the image to this point I was very happy that I shot the pigeon. I was only sorry that I hadn't shot more. I hadn't, so now I had to

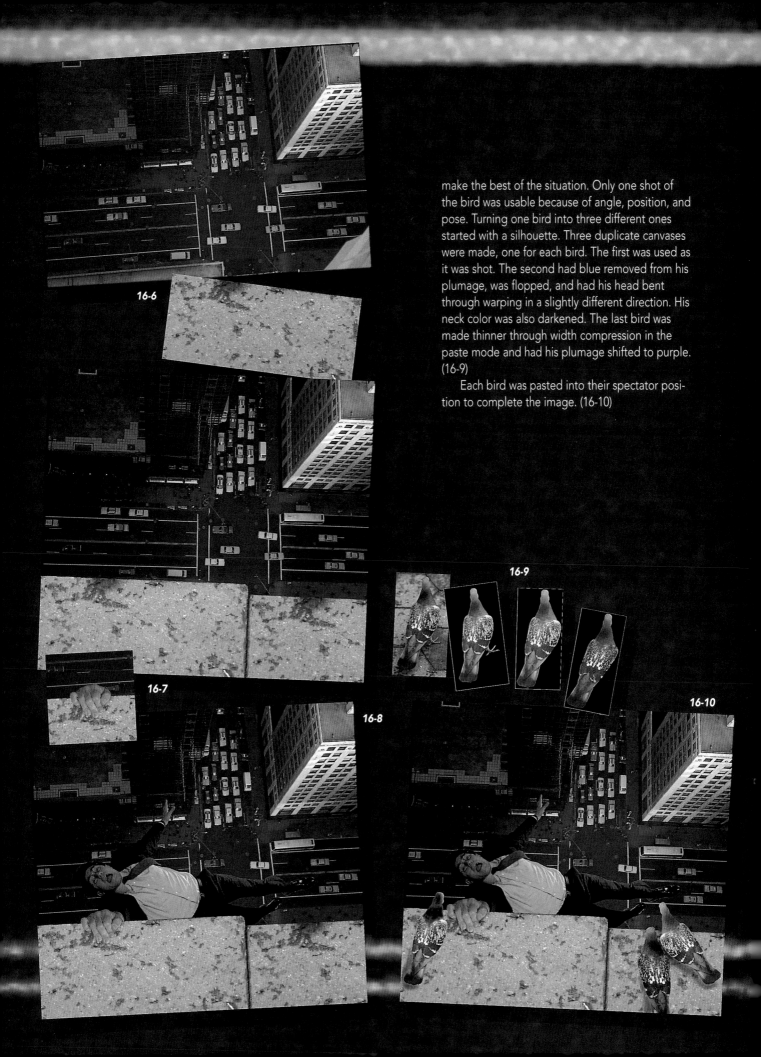

16-6

make the best of the situation. Only one shot of the bird was usable because of angle, position, and pose. Turning one bird into three different ones started with a silhouette. Three duplicate canvases were made, one for each bird. The first was used as it was shot. The second had blue removed from his plumage, was flopped, and had his head bent through warping in a slightly different direction. His neck color was also darkened. The last bird was made thinner through width compression in the paste mode and had his plumage shifted to purple. (16-9)

Each bird was pasted into their spectator position to complete the image. (16-10)

16-9

16-7

16-8

16-10

17

SLICE

IMAGE OF CASCADING REFRESHMENT

This exercise in conceptual visual communication was to make the consumer identify with and comprehend the meaning of, on a gestalt level, the descriptive phrases "clear as a mountain stream, natural as a sylvan forest, and total refreshment" as they relate to the product.

What is better on a steamy hot day than a swim in a pool fed by a mountain stream surrounded by a lush verdant forest? The source of all this refreshment is, naturally, the product pouring like a waterfall that forms a cascading series of smaller falls until it empties into a sparkling glass pool. In that pool are two beneficiaries of Slice's refreshing qualities with which the consumer can identify.

Finding the right location is always a problem. In this case, it was finding a series of waterfalls that could be made to look as if they were linked, and in a setting that was open enough to have a large version of the product tucked in the tops of the trees. Locating a natural pool that was large enough for a couple of models and small enough to capture its shape in a single shot was not easy either. A location scout suggested Dingman's Falls in northern New Jersey. It turned out to be perfect. It not only had a variety of falls but a pool fed by a waterfall, too. Shooting all of the outdoor scenes at one time meant that the lighting and the fauna would be consistent. Loosely translated, it was easier to put together. Although the day of the shoot was overcast, the flat lighting could be corrected later on the computer. (17-1)

The product container and the glass of the effervescent product were shot in the studio. Sparkling liquid is always tricky to shoot. The turbulence and the amount of bubbles were directly related to the force of the poor. Short duration strobe heads were placed to the right and left bottom of the glass. It was shot against a black background to clearly define the bubbles for later masking. (17-2)

To keep the liquid pouring continuously and evenly, a hole was punched in the bottom of the can and the liquid was poured through a funnel that was connected to the hole by a hose. (17-3)

A blue sky with white tufted clouds, never available when you need them, was taken from my stock file of skies. (17-4)

A long shot of the main falls seemed like a logical place to start. It literally became the foundation for the entire image without much modification at this point, aside from cropping. The tree tops were the perfect cradle for the can of Slice and enough space for the arc of the pour from can to the base of the falls. (17-5)

A second canvas, identical in size to the first, was opened and the main falls image was pasted onto it, too. The second shot of the smaller step falls was pasted in a position that aligned

17-1

17-2

17-3

logically to the main falls. For compositional consideration, it was necessary to have the flow of the liquid come around from left to right. The trees in the second shot were blended with the dense forest of the first image through cloning. To integrate the two images of the falls, every trace of the edge of the frame of the second shot had to be eliminated. Where the trees that overhung the step falls extended up and out of the frame, leaves and limbs had to be added to give the scene a natural look. This was accomplished by cloning and cutting out sections of the trees, and pasting them in appropriate positions. These cuts were then blended with cloning and restoring parts of the first image back into the second. Parts of the first falls image were restored back into the composited falls image from the first canvas. This served to connect the main falls in the background with the step

17-4

falls that moved into the foreground. Shrubs and trees were restored and added here, too. (17-6)

Once again a full size canvas, identical in size to the others, was created, and this time the second (or composite) canvas was duplicated on it. After silhouetting the glass by using the line art capability to outline its shape and filling the shape with the mask, the background was deleted. The silhouetted glass was then placed at the base of the step falls and pasted down. To connect the glass to the scene and make it a part of the action, the falls were restored around the back rim of the glass with some transparency to give the impression that the water is truly running over the lip of the glass. (17-7)

Nestling the glass into the rocks and making it an integral part of the scene was imperative to complete the allegory of the glass of Slice being synonymous with all that the rest of the visual implies. To accomplish this, the rocks at the base of the step falls were extended over the front of the glass on the left and extended down behind the glass on the right. A cut out of the rocks on the right was made and warped to follow the

17-5

17-6

17-7

contour of the glass on the right, then in the paste mode airbrushed onto the glass with approximately eight percent opacity to subtly create the illusion of a reflection.

Removing the sky from behind anything as detailed as the leaves of a stand of trees, in a convincing way, would have been an almost impossible feat before computers were introduced to the imaging process. The chrome key masking facility was used to create a mask of the flat gray sky. Inverting the mask masked the trees, enabling the sky to be deleted. (17-8)

With the mask over the trees still in place, a blue sky with white tufted clouds was inserted into the space that the former gray sky had occupied by pasting it over the masked trees. To give the scene a sunny appearance, the mask was inverted again and the trees were color shifted by adding yellow to the green leaves of the trees in the color correction module using selective color correction. A blurring brush was run over the edges of the tree tops to soften the merging of the leaves with the sky. (17-9)

17-10

17-9

17-8

17-11

17-12

To combine the image of the models swimming and sitting on the edge of the pool with the image of the scene containing the glass, the restore function—the ability to paint parts of one canvas onto another—was used frequently. First another canvas was created with the current image pasted on it. Over that image in its proportional size and place, the image of the two models by the falls was pasted down. Using a small airbrush tool, the previous image was restored around the model sitting on the rocks, including the glass rim between his legs. The two models were then painted into the previous canvas with the restore function going the opposite way, from new canvas to previous canvas. At this point, both waterfalls, the one in the shot with the models and the one flowing over the edge of the glass, were combined. The turbulence of the falls was combined with the turbulence of the pouring soda into the glass (the original image) and the effervescence of the soda in the glass. (17-10)

The source of all this refreshment, the product, was the next step in building the image. For something cold to look refreshing on a hot day, nothing can beat the cliché of condensation on the surface of the glass, can, or bottle. By isolating a single bubble in the glass I was able to use it to paint, in the paste-up mode, condensation wherever it needed to be seen. The condensation trails and the drop forming on the bottom of the can were painted with a palette created from various points in the image.

A luminance mask, which uses the lights and darks of an image to determine the amount of density, was created from the pour. A line art mask was made around the can and joined with luminance mask of the pour. Once the masks were made, the black background was deleted. (17-11)

The trees around the main waterfall were cloned to cover most of the waterfall, leaving just enough to create the splash and spray where the pour hit. The can was then pasted into the treetops, and the pour extended into what was left of the main falls. From a palette created from colors in the sky, the trees, and the white foam of the falls, the pour was painted in around the luminance mask. A clear liquid such as water acts as a lens and has no color qualities of its own. Whatever color is seen is a reflection from, or a transmission through the liquid. The splash at the bottom of the pour was created by painting with the cloning brush drawn from the waterfall's white water. (17-12)

18

SEAGRAMS SEVEN

"SEVENTH HEAVEN"
MAGAZINE ADVERTISEMENT

Every visual concept is built around accepted symbolic representations that encapsulate the main idea: diamonds for wealth, forests and lakes for nature, and in this case, a blue sky and white tufted clouds for heaven. The challenge in this ad was not to take a photograph of something but to make a photograph of something, a sky, and change it into something else while maintaining its photographic integrity. In other words, find a sky with clouds that could be sculpted into the Seagrams Seven logo.

Finding the right sky was not an easy task. Between the skies that are stored in the files of the major stock agencies and what I have in my own stock collection of skies, there were thousands to look at. Unfortunately, it was even more difficult to describe to the stock photo agencies exactly what I was looking for. The request went something like this: "Please send me all the skies that you have that has a cloud that looks like a seven."

The response was usually, "A what?" Fortunately, I had just the right sky in my collection. I was on an assignment in Florida, and while waiting for the sun to set, I shot this one for my files with a camera that I always carry with me for personal or stock shots.

18-1

It was like a block of marble that had the vague shape of the object that the sculptor wanted to sculpt. (18-1)

Auguste Rodin, the sculptor, once responded to an inquiry as to how he would go about sculpting an elephant out of a block of marble. "What I would do," he said, "is cut away the parts of the block that didn't look like an elephant." After making the blank canvas to the size of the ad with additional room for bleed, I pasted the selected sky in place. (18-2)

Next, I made an accurate tracing of the Seagrams Seven logo in line art. I drew the layout in line art and indicated where the type and the small product shot would go. In this form, they were both available for use as overlays in the construction of the image. (18-3)

Two canvases of identical size, the size of the ad with bleed, were created and the layout of the logo was placed over them. The same cropped image of the original sky was pasted down on them. (18-4)

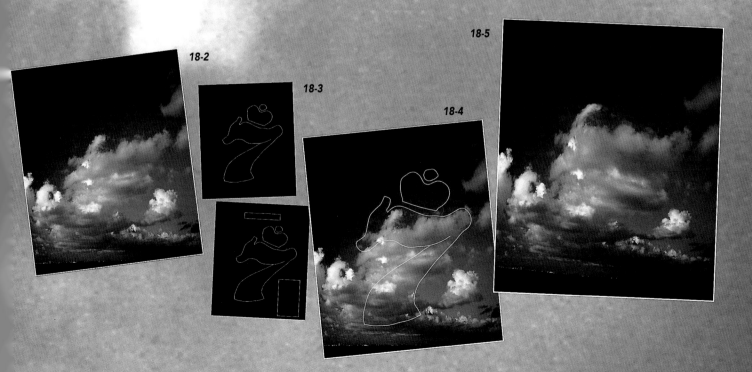

18-5

18-2

18-3

18-4

A cut was made of the top part of the main cloud. This cut was tilted upright in the paste mode and repositioned to fit the sketch of the logo. The cloning brush was used to blend the paste up with the rest of the sky. (18-5)

The cloning brush was used to fill in the balance of the shape at the top of the seven and define it more clearly. This was accomplished by picking up parts of the clouds that matched in color and texture and transferring them to the areas of the seven that needed to be filled in. By cloning the blue sky behind the clouds and painting it over the parts of the clouds to be eliminated, the curved spine began to take shape. (18-6)

Cloning tools or brushes are used to transfer one part of the photographic image to another part of the image by painting it with whatever size and kind of brush is appropriate. Most impressive of all is that the entire piece of the image including all the nuances of texture, softness, and shifting color is transferred, too. This tool is also responsible for the demise of the skilled traditional retouchers with their dyes and bleaches.

To complete the delineation of the rest of the seven, a blue background was painted over the rest of the clouds that didn't contribute to its shape. Additional highlights were added to the clouds to give the seven volume. All the manipulation and construction was with the cloning tool in the airbrush configuration. (18-7)

In addition to further defining the shape of the seven, the creation of the crown was begun by cloning parts of clouds from the base of the seven and surrounding clouds. To make the Seagram's logo pop, some of the surrounding clouds were darkened. By making a duplicate and darkening it in the color correction module, I was able to combine the lighter and darker versions to create shadows or make them recede under other elements in the layout. (18-8)

Once the crown was completed, it was impossible to tell the crown clouds from the original clouds and the image was ready for output. (18-9)

18-9

18-8

18-7

18-6

19

TECHNICS

CATALOGUE COVER

Although the catalogue covers the complete line of consumer electronic entertainment products, the client wanted to feature the latest top of the line audio and video products and build around them the atmosphere and excitement that today's home entertainment centers can provide. The art director supplied a very tight comp to follow.

This assignment involved a great many components. Some were supplied by the client, but most of the images were created by me for this cover illustration.

Casting the right model to visually represent a specific musical genre is always a challenge given the subjective quality of image stereotyping. To represent classical music, what better than a renaissance-like cherub? For jazz, a trumpet player was appropriate. Rock music is synonymous with the electric guitar and long hair. It has also been known to over-stimulate teenagers. Each model was shot against a neutral gray background to make the silhouetting process easier. (19-1)

The two product shots were supplied by the client. Getting the cables to arc gracefully in three different curves required the use of very thin monofilament fishing line to hold them in position. (19-2)

Angel wings are not that easy to come by on earth so they were supplied by a model maker. Because the image was being assembled on computer, it was only necessary to have one made and not worry about how to attach it to the little girl who was to wear it. White tufted clouds, which were to act as a unifying element in the composition, came from my stock files of skies, and the stock photo of the jets were supplied by the client. The sci-fi illustrations of the robot and space station were also supplied by the client. (19-3)

Because of the complexity of the composition, a tight line tracing of the comp was necessary for the placement of the elements. In the computer, it's possible to use the tracing like an overlay that can be turned on and off at will. (19-4)

Each element in the composition had to be silhouetted on an empty background in order to make it possible to lay one object over the next without visual contamination. The products, a receiver with remote and a projection television,

19-1

19-2

19-3

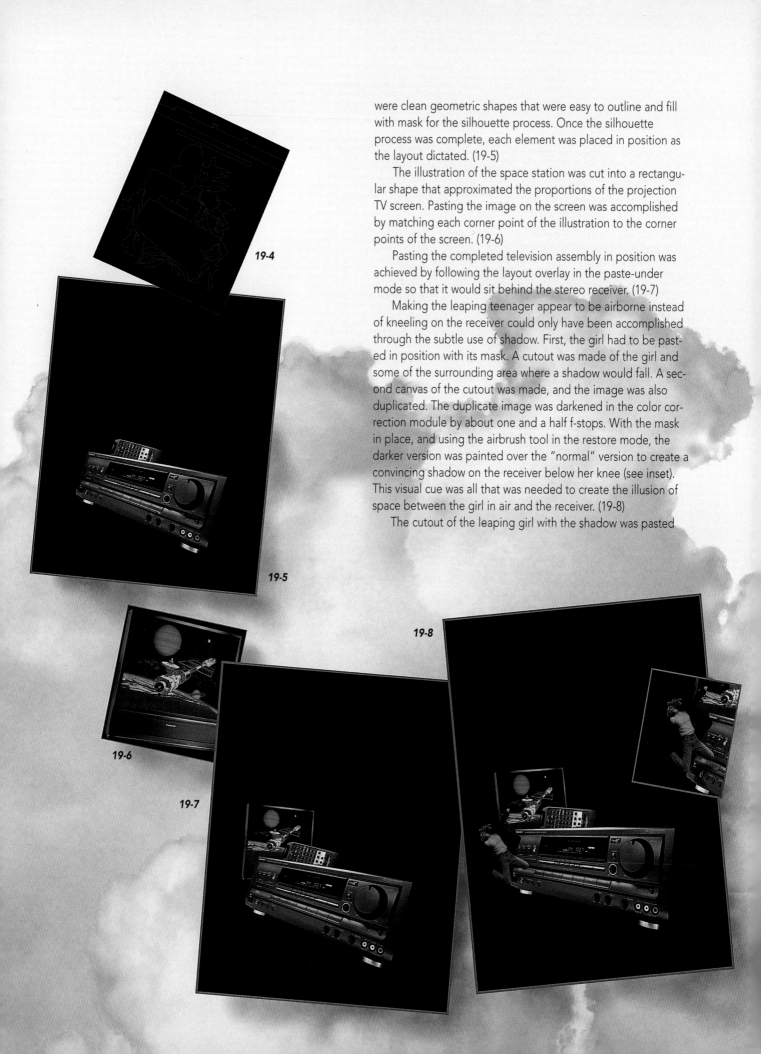

were clean geometric shapes that were easy to outline and fill with mask for the silhouette process. Once the silhouette process was complete, each element was placed in position as the layout dictated. (19-5)

The illustration of the space station was cut into a rectangular shape that approximated the proportions of the projection TV screen. Pasting the image on the screen was accomplished by matching each corner point of the illustration to the corner points of the screen. (19-6)

Pasting the completed television assembly in position was achieved by following the layout overlay in the paste-under mode so that it would sit behind the stereo receiver. (19-7)

Making the leaping teenager appear to be airborne instead of kneeling on the receiver could only have been accomplished through the subtle use of shadow. First, the girl had to be pasted in position with its mask. A cutout was made of the girl and some of the surrounding area where a shadow would fall. A second canvas of the cutout was made, and the image was also duplicated. The duplicate image was darkened in the color correction module by about one and a half f-stops. With the mask in place, and using the airbrush tool in the restore mode, the darker version was painted over the "normal" version to create a convincing shadow on the receiver below her knee (see inset). This visual cue was all that was needed to create the illusion of space between the girl in air and the receiver. (19-8)

The cutout of the leaping girl with the shadow was pasted

19-4

19-5

19-6

19-7

19-8

over the cover image replacing the girl without the shadow. Next in order was the silhouette of the jazz musician. (19-9)

In the same way that the figures in the photographs were silhouetted and pasted into position, the robot was cut out of the larger illustration that originally contained it and, silhouetted, became a component in this one. Using the airbrush tool in the paint mode at a moderate transparency setting, the glow and star burst were added to the muzzle of the gun that the robot carried to merge the illustration with the rest of the cover image. (19-10)

By cutting and silhouetting each wire separately, I was able to manipulate individual colors. Using the color correction module, I was able to use the tonal value range of the gray color, from highlight to shadow, and impose it onto the color of each wire. An opacity mask was used to protect the metallic tip color and band of each wire from the color changes that were taking place in the rest of the wire. Once the color issues were dealt with, the wires were pasted, one over the other, into the composition. (19-11)

Converting an adorable, earthbound little girl into a semi-diaphanous angel had to be accomplished after the component was pasted into the final composition. The area that she occu-

19-9

19-10

19-11

pied was cut out to conserve memory and time while working. It is a lot quicker and less memory intensive to work on a smaller canvas than a very a large one, like the 225 megabyte file of this image.

The silhouette of the girl was pasted in position using the under mode to place her behind the audio unit and remote control. She was rotated to the left to make it look like she was resting her elbow on the unit. It is this interrelationship between components that integrate all the elements into a single unit. (19-12)

First the right wing was pasted into position using the under mode to place it behind her back. Care was taken to make sure the wing worked harmoniously with the rest of the composition. Since the wings had to appear to be symmetrical, the second wing had to be seen, and therefore had to be at an angle that would work on both sides of her

body for the shot. The wing was flipped in the computer and pasted in the under mode so as to make it appear as if it, too, was growing out of her back. (19-13)

A large airbrush tool, set for medium transparency, was used to give the girl and her wings a soft glow. Starting with an outline around the edges of her image, I then began to fill in the interior parts of her body and wings with a lighter touch. This completed the effect of the glow emanating from inside the angel. The remote control and the receiver were masked to keep them from being affected by the glow. (19-14)

Having completed the effect on the angel, the cutout was pasted in position, adding another component to the final piece. (19-15)

The rock star was the next element in the lineup. Silhouetting the frizzy hair became a great challenge. First I

19-12

19-13

19-14

used a chrome key masking tool on one small section at a time. It looked pretty ragged when I finished, but the head was silhouetted on an empty background. This ragged look led to the second step. I picked out several colors from his hair to set up a menu and then painted and smoothed the hair completely around his head. When the image of the rock star was completed, it was added to the rest of the composition. (19-16)

Top Gun, the movie on surround sound video tape, was the most popular demonstration of this capability in home entertainment. It was, therefore, logical to use a visual trigger of the exciting entertainment experience by including jet fighters as part of the total image. After silhouetting the planes, they were pasted down in the under mode, which put them behind the rock star and his guitar. (19-17)

To tie the complex unit together as a single design element, the art director wanted to use white cumulous clouds. The effect was to create a visual island floating on a page of white. I started by isolating and silhouetting small individual cloud formations from the stock shot selected from my files. Some of the formations were created by cloning parts of other clouds onto existing ones, and others were created by piecing several parts together to form new shapes. (19-18)

Many had to be lightened. Against a deep blue or black sky they looked white, but against a solid white page they

19-17

19-16

19-15

turned several shades of medium gray. A white background was added to several formations, to evaluate the relative whiteness of the clouds against a pure white background. (19-19)

A new canvas was created to the size of the cover on which the final art would appear. The assembly was traced and reduced to the size that it would appear on the cover. Using the master sketch as a guide, the clouds were sized and pasted in positions that would accomplish the unifying task for which they were chosen or created. (19-20)

To create the final assembly that would become the cover, a second canvas was created, and the clouds in their final position were pasted on it to duplicate the first canvas. The assembly was sized to match the sketch and pasted down on the first canvas. (19-21) A white background was painted behind the assembled composition. The clouds from the second canvas were painted, in the restore mode, over the assembled art on the first canvas where they were needed to blend with the jazz musician and the wires in an effort to keep them from looking like pasted cutouts in its final form.

19-18

19-19

19-20

19-21

20

APOLLO SOFTWARE

MAGAZINE ADVERTISEMENT

With the introduction of computers and reservation software for the travel industry came an opportunity to sell advantageous positioning. If a hotel or car rental agency wanted to be one of the first names the travel agent saw when he or she logged onto their computer for a hotel or car rental in a particular city, they could pay for an ad placement in an up front premium position. The concept is very much like paying to have the inside or back cover of a magazine for an advertisement, where prominent positioning promises the product is most likely to be noticed. To communicate this idea to potential advertisers, the art director wanted a representative symbol for the hotel industry to burst through the computer screen for an in-your-face can't miss it look.

In every assembly, there is always one component that will set the tone or look for the entire image, either becauseit is a stock image, or it is a situation with limited control over the way it must be photgraphed. The building had to be a generic hotel-looking building and there had to be a vantage point high enough and close enough to shoot from the point of view of someone looking at the computer screen. After three days of scouting, the almost ideal location was found. The building was too tall to use in its entirety, but its architectural design allowed me to create a credible design to finish off the top of the building. I had to wait for the sun to be in the correct position for it to be lit appropriately, without what would be strange shadows cast by the surrounding buildings. To exaggerate the perspective, ad drama, and include as much of

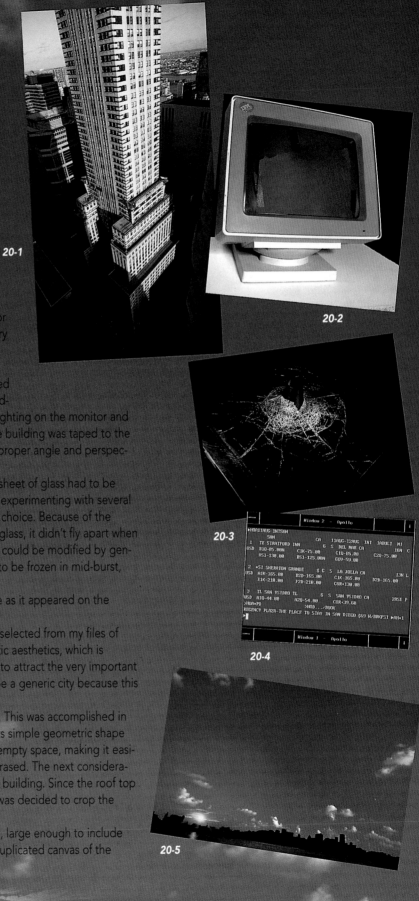

20-1

20-2

20-3

20-4

20-5

the building as possible, to increase my options for cropping later, the building was shot with a very wide angle curve-linear distortion-free lens. (20-1)

Once the building was shot, the lighting and angle of view was established for the other affected component, the computer monitor. Since the building was to emerge from the monitor screen, the lighting on the monitor and the building had to be consistent. A tracing of the building was taped to the ground glass of the camera to help establish the proper angle and perspective of the building relative to the monitor. (20-2)

To create the bursting through glass effect, a sheet of glass had to be shattered, but its shape had to be retained. After experimenting with several different kinds of glass, safety plate glass was the choice. Because of the membrane laminated between the two sheets of glass, it didn't fly apart when it shattered and it maintained its shape. Its shape could be modified by gently pushing on its center, and because it appears to be frozen in mid-burst, the lighting could be carefully set up. (20-3)

The screen grab of listings in the real software as it appeared on the screen was supplied by the client. (20-4)

A sunset of a generic city from the water was selected from my files of stock photos. The sunset was selected for dramatic aesthetics, which is important for any vacation. A cityscape was used to attract the very important business traveler to the travel industry. It had to be a generic city because this was a national trade ad. (20-5)

First the building had to be silhouetted. This was accomplished in the line art mode by drawing an outline around its simple geometric shape and filling it with mask. To float the silhouette in empty space, making it easier to work with, the rest of the photograph was erased. The next consideration in the building shot was where to top off the building. Since the roof top views of buildings show off their ugliest areas, it was decided to crop the building just above eye level. (20-6)

A cutout was made of the top of the building, large enough to include the area that was to be modified and a backup duplicated canvas of the

20-6

20-7

20-8

cutout was made to restore any modification that was unacceptable. A mask of the center vertical shape was created by using the line art capability. An outline, starting with the upper-most floor that would be left in its original form and then down to the base of the building, was made, filled with mask, and added to the first vertical mask. A cutout of the next floor was made and pasted down one window in from its original configuration. This created a stepped look. This floor was then masked and joined to the larger mask. The identical process was repeated twice more on the right side to give the top of the building a decorative look. In order to finish off the top of the building, the decorative space between the floors was cut out and used repeatedly to give it a solid realistic cap. (20-7a) A similar process was done to the floors on the far or left side to give the building a symmetrically tapered look. (20-7b)

Before the modified cutout could be pasted back into its original position on the cropped building, the parts that would have stuck out were erased. The cutout of the upper part of the building was then pasted in its original position creating a new generic hotel-looking building that doesn't exist. (20-8)

Masking the shattering glass was tricky because the only parts of the glass to maintain opacity were the edges of the pieces and the rest had to appear transparent.

Making a chrome key mask of the black color seemed the most logical first step. This removed the background, but it also removed the more contrasting separations between the pieces caused by refraction. Those had to be painted back in by hand, a task made easier by reversing the chrome key mask. (20-9)

The next step was to silhouette parts of the shattering glass image into individual transparent shards. Since the glass was already silhouetted, it was simply a question of picking the pieces that had the most interesting shapes and cutting them out to create a file of shards to be created for later use. Once the shards were silhouetted, in paste-up with the warping capability, they could be transformed into many other shapes. Each shape had a visual function such as speed or fragmentation. (20-10)

To symbolize the computerized aspect of travel reservation, it was decided to use just the frame of the monitor and its screen. The entire monitor would become dated more quickly. The shape of the frame was masked with line art inside and out. When the unmasked area was erased, only the frame remained. In the paint mode, the cloning brush was used to paint over the logo or trademark as well as any dirt, scratches, or stains that weren't removed or couldn't be fixed before the shoot. (20-11)

The image of the shattering glass was picked up and, with the frame mask still in place, pasted down where the

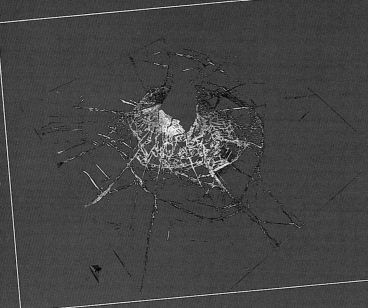

20-9

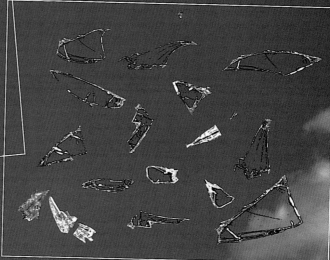

20-10

20-11

20-12

screen would have been. To make the shattering screen look real, two considerations had to be addressed. The first was to make the perspective of the screen match the perspective of the monitor frame. This was accomplished in the paste-up mode with the perspective correction capability. Using the edge of the frame as a guide, the edge of the glass image was matched to it. Once the match was completed, the perspective of the screen and the perspective of the frame were identical. Sizing and cropping the glass image to fit the screen were easy at this point. The second consideration was the slight curvature of the screen around the edges and the need to pull the center of the screen outward as would logically happen if the building was actually pushing through. This second manipulation was done with the warping capability making the grid overlay conform to the inside shape of the frame. Then by grabbing the inside gridlines near the center and pulling them out, the glass image followed. (20-12)

A duplicate canvas of the monitor frame with the shattered glass in it was created. This second duplicate image was used later to restore the shattered glass around the building after it was pasted down. The building was picked up in paste-up mode and positioned over the point of penetration through the monitor screen on the first canvas. It was necessary to rotate the building to make the direction and energy of the thrust more accu-

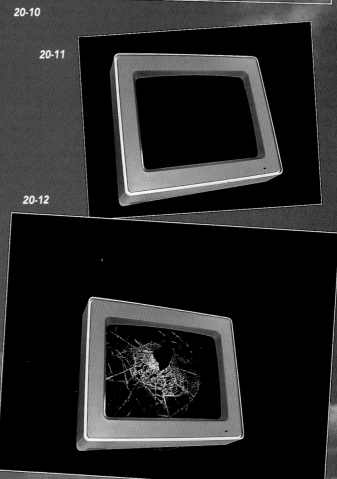

rately match the perspective and dynamics of the monitor. A third canvas was created from the first canvas after the building had been pasted into position. This canvas was used to combine the building and the glass. It was necessary to use a third canvas for the restoring back and forth between the building, the shattering glass, and the shards because the nuances and subtleties required a great deal of trial and error until it worked properly.

Once the building and the glass were satisfactorily combined so that it appeared to come through the glass, it was time to introduce the shards. Shards are the loose fragments, the glass shrapnel, that an impact of this kind would have produced. In addition to the visual explosive effect that shards give to the image, they also create excitement in the form of motion, and aid in the composition by creating arrows for the eye to follow. Since the individual pieces were already silhouetted and transparent, it was just a matter of placing them. (20-13)

Once the merging of the building and the glass was complete, the display on the monitor had to be added. The actual software display that most travel agents are familiar with was supplied by the client. To create the correct perspective of the screen display and have it fit the monitor screen, the perspective correction capability of the paste up module was once again brought into play. By matching the perspective of the edges of the display to the edges of the frame around the screen, the perspective was consistent. Another duplicate canvas, this time to size with the display pasted in position but on top of the glass, was created. The display was also pasted under the assembled image; because the shattered glass was already transparent the display was clearly

visible through it. By using the restore function, additional parts of the display were painted in from the display pasted on the duplicate canvas. (20-14)

To complete the image, several sunsets were pulled from my stock collection. Another canvas, the final size of the ad, was created. The selected sunset was cropped and pasted onto the canvas. The assembled screen, building, and display were pasted over the sky in position, allowing for the headline and copy as the layout dictated. (20-15)

After the monitor was in position, additional shards were pasted at strategic and aesthetic points on the final image. Some were blurred and some were streaked as the need became evident. A second version also included a car and plane to indicate that other booked services could take advantage of this new feature. Because the original image and components were saved, the addition of the other elements and relocating and flopping of the generic hotel was not a problem.

20-15

20-14

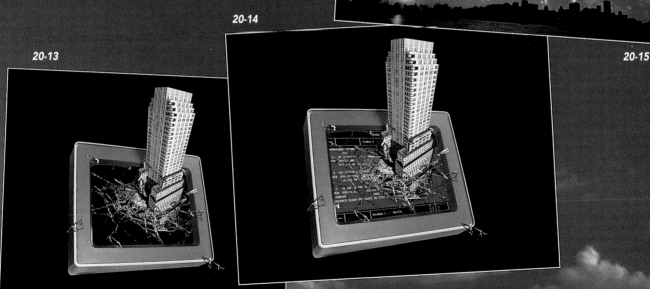

20-13

Gallery

A COLLECTION OF IMAGES CREATED
BY BARRY BLACKMAN

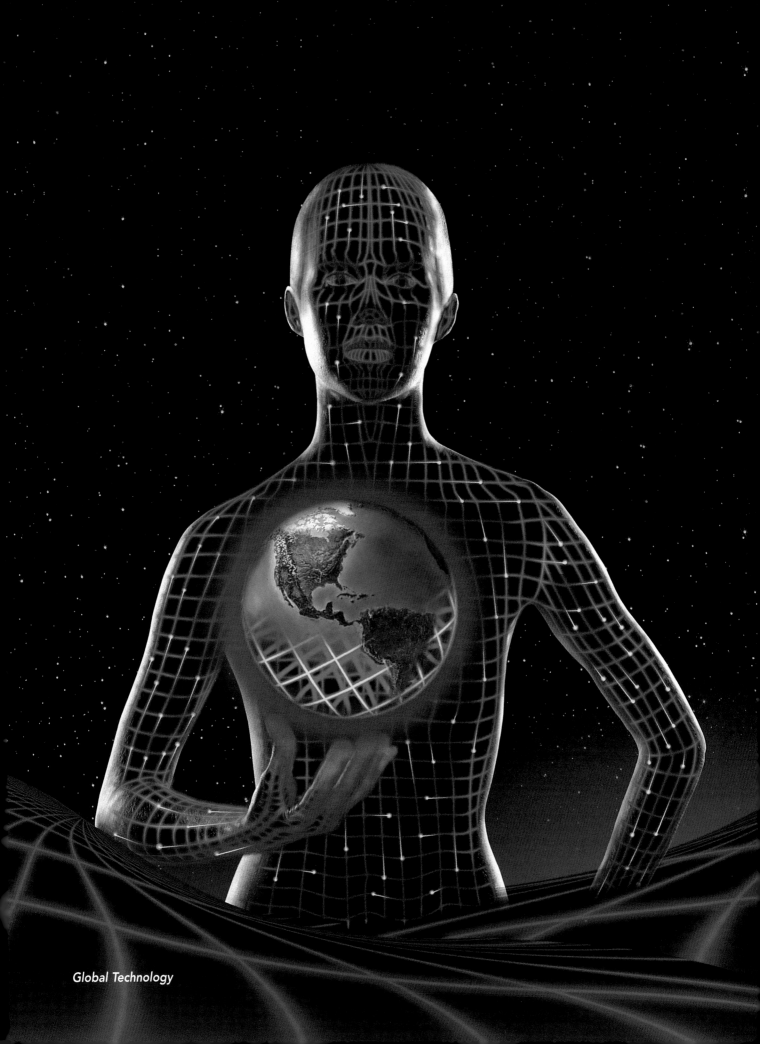

Global Technology

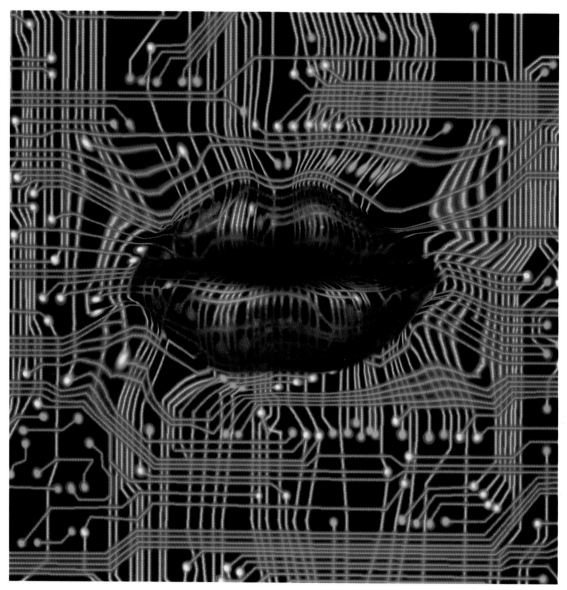

Hot Lips (above)

Barrio Lovers (facing page)
Hardware/Software Network Packaging (following pages, left)
What's Next? (following pages, right)

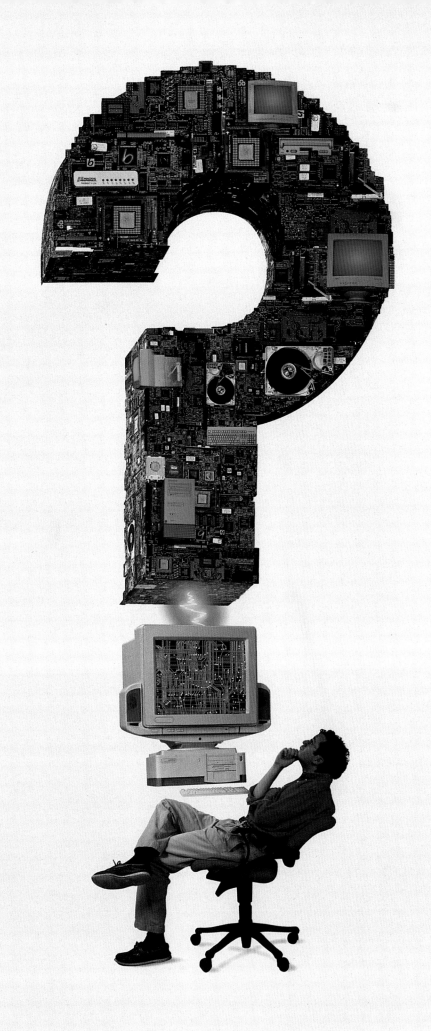

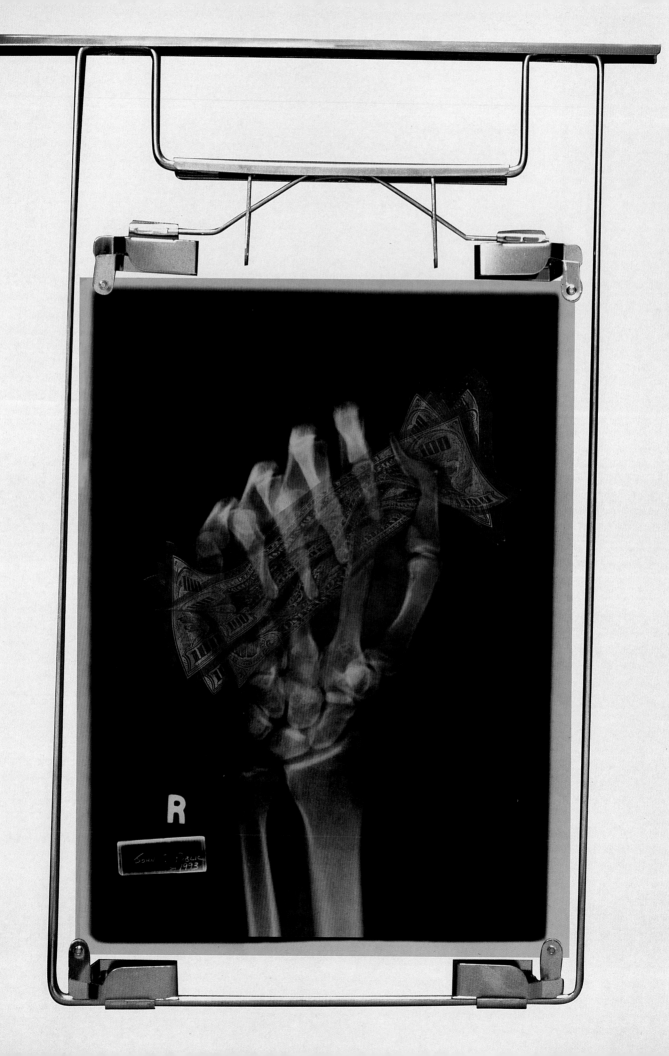

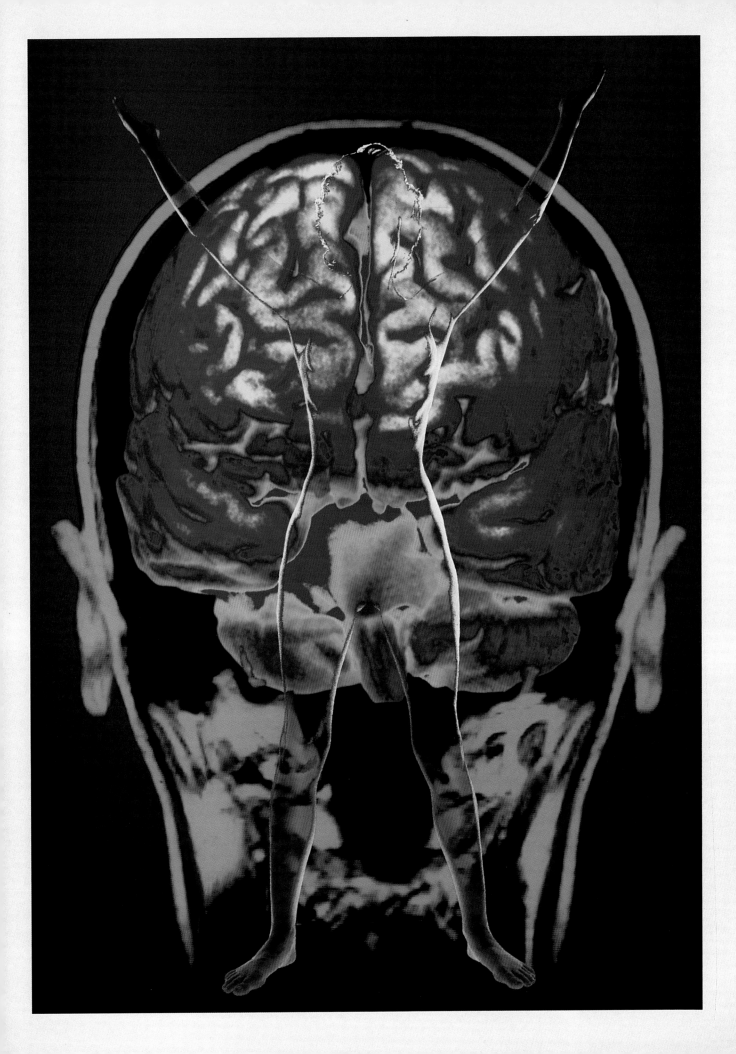

Medicine—A Fist Full of Dollars (preceding pages, left)
Mind Over Matter (preceding pages, right)

A Beastly Cold (above)

Oh, That Wrung Out Feeling (facing page)

Economic States

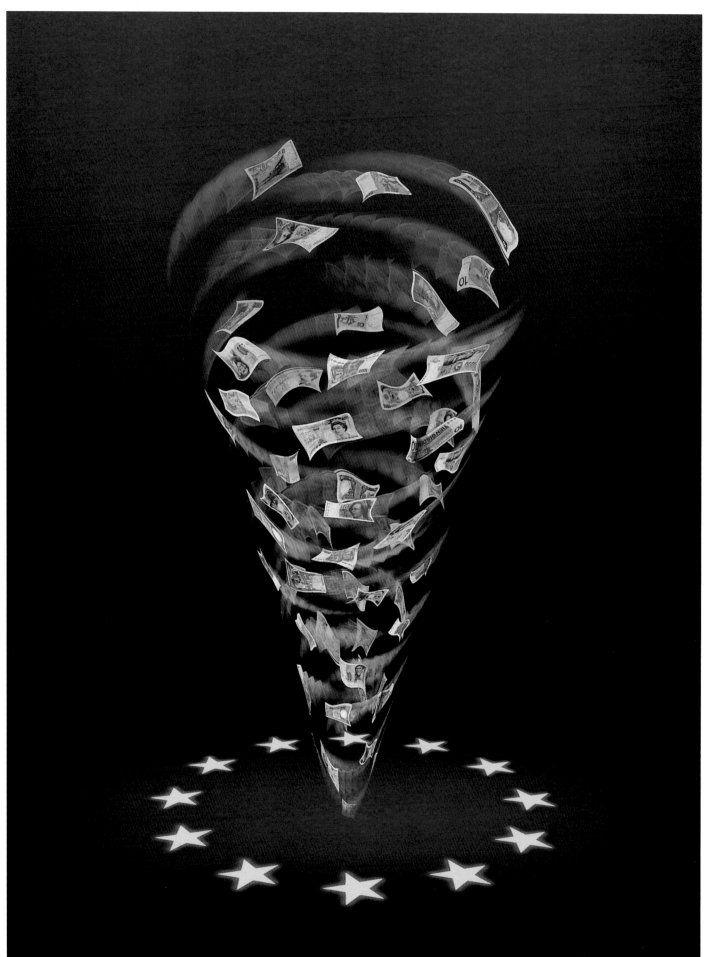

Common Market Currency Tempest

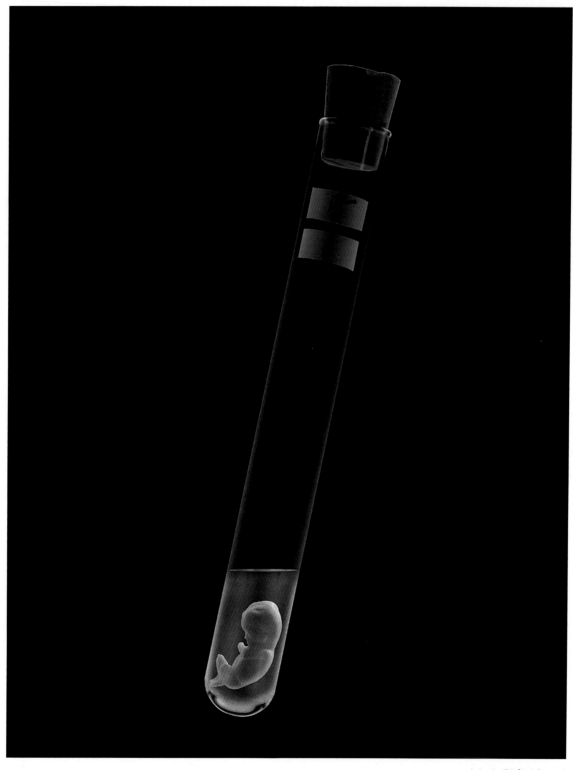

It's A Girl! (above)

Bun in the Oven (facing page)

A two thousand head portrait
of
PRESIDENT CLINTON

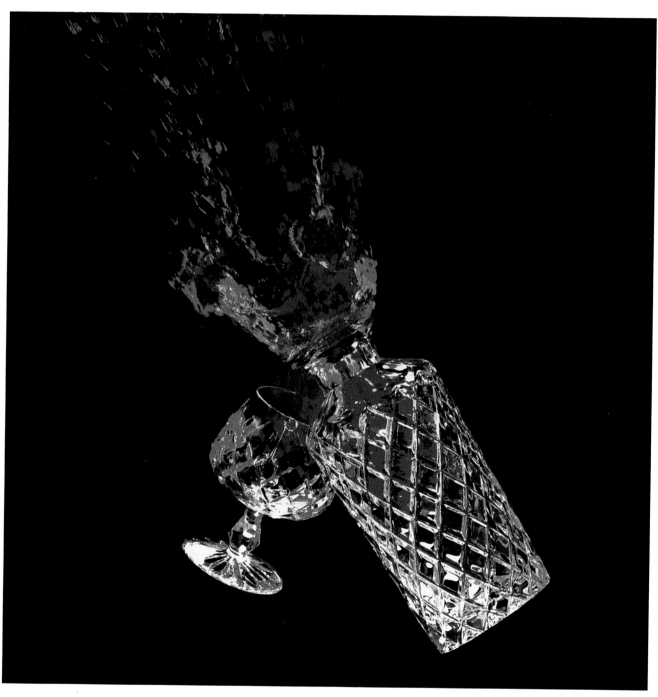

Crystal Splash (above)

Celebration Time (facing page)

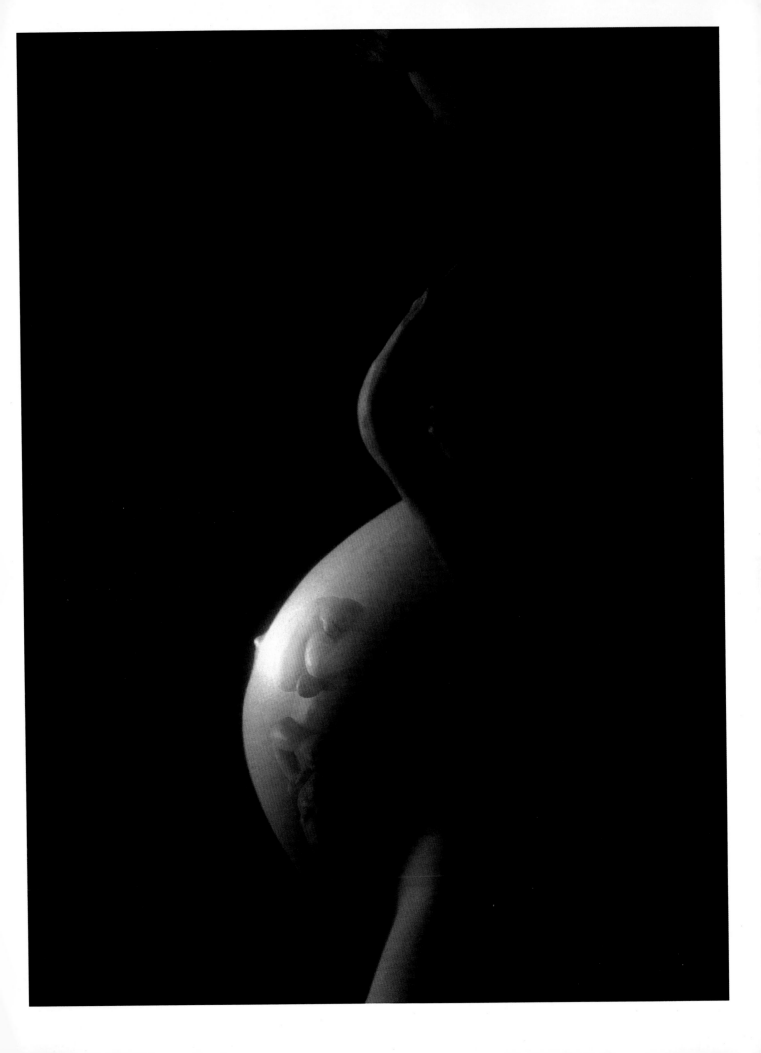

Chemical Waste

Global Meltdown (facing page)
Global Warming (following pages, left)
Time is Running Out (following pages, right)

Get That Last Drop

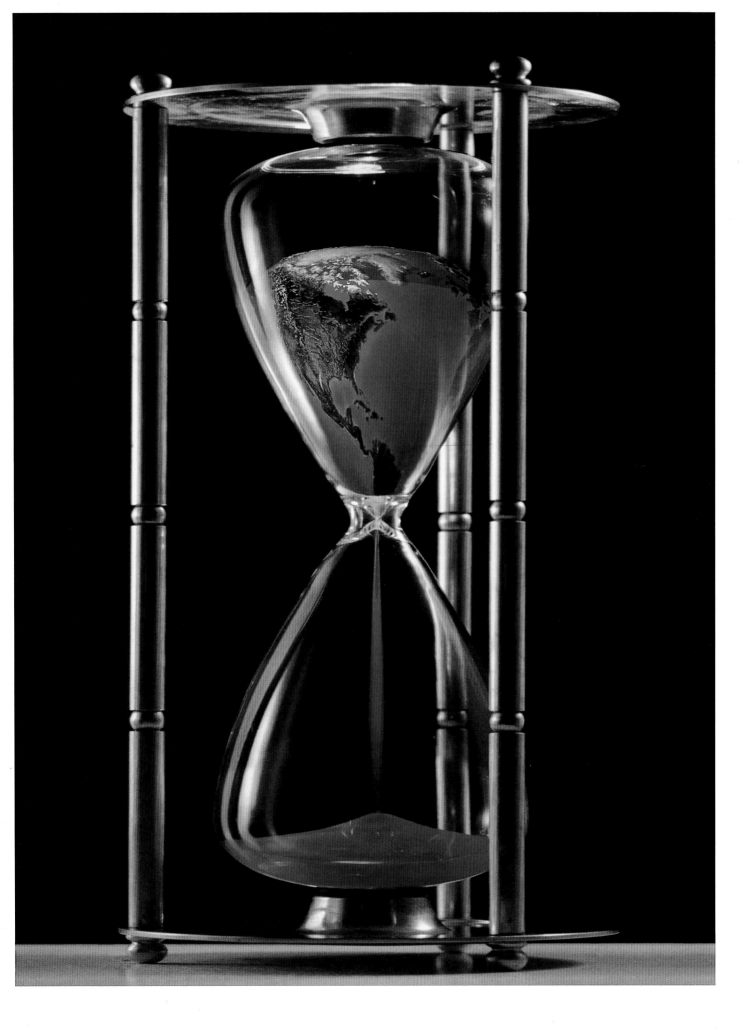

To Die For

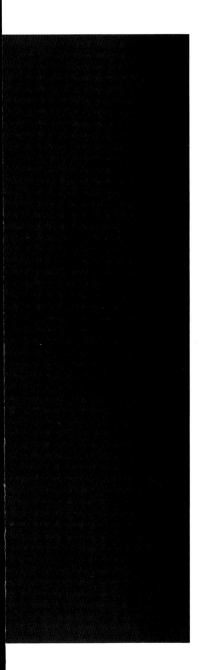

Short Sighted—Pollution

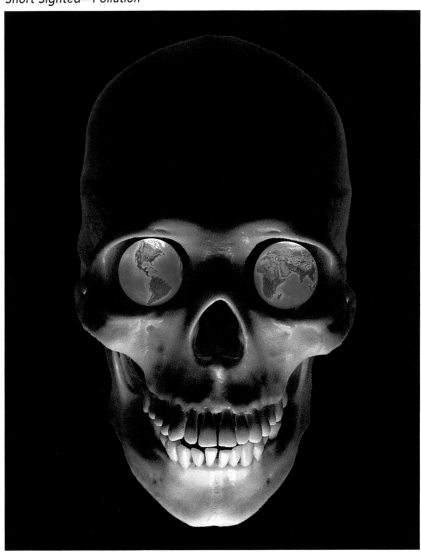

My Land

Dream Face

Bottle Baby

Bernie Nicholls as a Ranger

Signs (facing page)

Makeup

E.59 ST
PARK AV

← **ONE WAY**

NO STANDING
7 AM – 10 AM
4 PM – 7 PM
MON THRU FRI
←→

NO **PARKING**
7 AM – 7 PM
MON THRU FRI
→

E 59 ST

← ONE WAY

NO
COMMERCIAL
TRAFFIC

THE NEW YORK TIMES, THURSDAY, JUNE 30, 1983

New York Stock Exchange

CONSOLIDATED TRADING
WEDNESDAY, JUNE 29, 1983

Continued From Preceding Page

Stock Tables Explained

Rage (preceding pages)
No Contest (facing page)

Lady in the Lake

The Aging Process

Spiral Lips

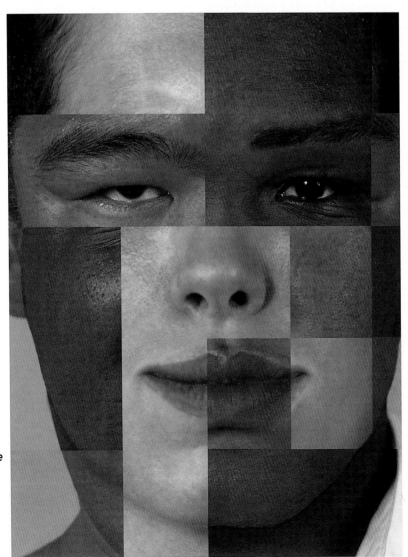

Race Face

Space Ball (preceding pages, left)
Light and Dry (preceding pages, right)

We're Back

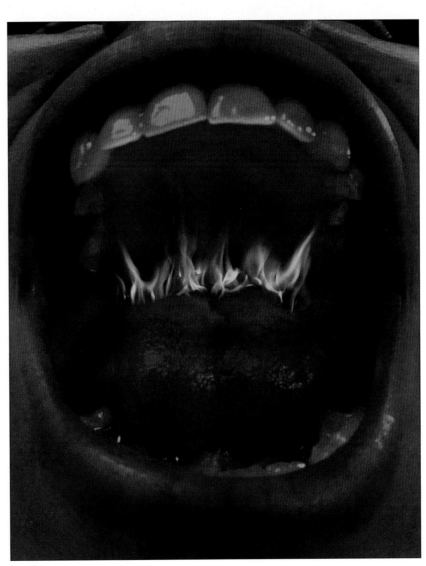

Hot Air

Fireball

Headache (facing page)

Sports Illustrated—"A Fan in the Year 2001"

Inspiration

Credits

Page 9: *Jurassic Park*, Amblin Entertainment, Steven Spielberg-director, ©1996 by Universal City Studios, Inc. Courtesy of MCA Publishing Rights, a Division of MCA Inc. All rights reserved. **Page 10:** *Seventh Seal*, Janus Repertory, Ingmar Bergman-director, courtesy of Janus Films. **Page 10:** *Satiracon*, United Artists Corporation, Frederico Fellini-director, ©1968 PEA Produzioni Europee Associates SAS. **Page 10:** *Persistence of Memory*, Museum of Modern Art, Salvador Dali-artist. **Page 11:** *Order's Friend*, Rene Magritte-artist. **Page 11:** *Sky and Water*, M.C. Escher-artist, ©1996 M.C. Escher/Cordon Art-Baarn-Holland. All rights reserved. **Page 12:** *untitled*, Jerry N. Uelsman-Photographer. **Page 26:** Scot Fletcher-art director; Don Bailey-art director. **Page 34:** David Loewy-art director, ©1992 CMP Publications Inc., reproduced from Varbusiness with permission. **Page 42:** Peter Comitini-senior art director; Pet scans (right and left), Medichrome-Howard Sochurek; Pet scans (top and bottom) Bruce Coleman-Alfred Pasieka, ©1992, Newsweek Inc. All rights reserved. Reprinted with permission. **Page 48:** Conrad Warre-art director, ©1990 *Discover* Magazine. Reprinted with permission. **Page 54:** Peter Comitini-senior art director; Ron Meyerson-senior editor, ©1992, Newsweek, Inc. All rights reserved. Reprinted with permission. **Page 60:** Jill Fangman-art director, reprinted by special permission from the Official Airline Guides. ©1996, Reed Travel Group. All rights reserved. **Page 68:** Steve Newman-art director. **Page 86:** Kristina Muller Eberhard-art director. **Page 92:** David Loewy-art director, ©1992 CMP Publications Inc., reproduced from Varbusiness with permission. **Page 98:** Tom Yohe-art director. **Page 106:** Frederick Rescott-art director. **Page 130:** Ross Sutherland-art director/creative director. **Page 134:** Frank Santelia-creative services manager; product photography (TV stereo equipment), Sam Calello-photographer; robot illustration, David Schleinkofer-artist; space station, Paul Alexander. **Page 151:** Fabien West-art director. **Page 154:** David Loewy-art director. **Page 155:** David Loewy-art director. **Page 156:** Peter Comitini-senior art director. **Page 157:** Richard Boddy-art director; MRI scan of skull-Larry Mulvehill. **Page 158:** Frederick Rescott-art director. **Pages 166 & 167:** Peter Comitini-art director. **Page 168:** Ron Meyerson-senior art director. **Page 170:** Jason Lee-art director. **Page 171:** Ron Meyerson-senior art director. **Pages 180-181:** Peter Comitini-senior art director. **Page 183 (top):** Steve Huffman-art director, inset photograph-Al Tielemans. **Page 183 (bottom):** Ross Buck-art director.